30-Minute Groups

RELATIONSHIPS AND BELONGING

VALUING SELF AND OTHERS, CREATING MEANINGFUL CONNECTIONS, AND SETTING HEALTHY BOUNDARIES

DR. AMY E. BALTIMORE, MEd, EdS, LPSC, NCC

NATIONAL CENTER for YOUTH ISSUES

Duplication and Copyright

No part of this publication may be reproduced, stored in a retrieval system, or transmitted in any form by any means, electronic, mechanical, photocopy, video or audio recording, or otherwise without prior written permission from the publisher, except for all worksheets and activities which may be reproduced for a specific group or class. Reproduction for an entire school or school district is prohibited.

NCYI titles may be purchased in bulk at special discounts for educational, business, fundraising, or promotional use. For more information, please email sales@ncyi.org.

NATIONAL CENTER for YOUTH ISSUES
P.O. Box 22185
Chattanooga, TN 37422-2185
423.899.5714 • 866.318.6294
fax: 423.899.4547 • www.ncyi.org

ISBN: 9781965066140
© 2025 National Center for Youth Issues, Chattanooga, TN
All rights reserved.
Written by: Dr. Amy E. Baltimore, MEd, EdS, LPSC, NCC
Published by National Center for Youth Issues
Printed in the U.S.A. • July 2025

Third party links are accurate at the time of publication, but may change over time.

The information in this book is designed to provide helpful information on the subjects discussed and is not intended to be used, nor should it be used, to diagnose or treat any mental health or medical condition. For diagnosis or treatment of any mental health or medical issue, consult a licensed counselor, psychologist, or physician. The publisher and author are not responsible for any specific mental or physical health needs that may require medical supervision, and are not liable for any damages or negative consequences from any treatment, action, application, or preparation, to any person reading or following the information in this book. References are provided for informational purposes only and do not constitute endorsement of any websites or other sources.

ASCA National Model®, Recognized ASCA Model Program® and RAMP® are registered trademarks of the American School Counselor Association. Our use of them does not imply an affiliation with or endorsement by the American School Counselor Association.

Contents

Introduction 4

    Introductory Group Session 8

Chapter 1: Understanding Your Strengths 10

Chapter 2: Appreciating the Value in Others 17

Chapter 3: Finding Where You Belong 26

Chapter 4: Achieving Wellness and Balance 34

Chapter 5: Defining Healthy Relationships 42

Chapter 6: Recognizing Unhealthy Relationships 52

Chapter 7: Protecting Your Worth 60

Chapter 8: Developing Consideration for Others 70

Chapter 9: Knowing Your Limits 80

Chapter 10: Respecting Others' Boundaries 89

Final Group Session 97

Action Plan 98

Relationships And Belonging Group Permission Form 99

Relationships And Belonging Group Expectations 100

Group Attendance Form 101

Group Attendance Form (Example) 102

Pre- and Post-Assessment 103

Results Report 104

Results Report (Example) 105

Certificate of Completion 106

Relationships and Belonging Group Completion Letter 107

References 108

About the Author 109

Amy's Sessions 110

30-Minute Groups 111

About NCYI 112

Introduction

Social interaction is the foundation of how students learn and grow. Things like their culture, how they communicate (language), and their interactions with others deeply influence their learning journey. In fact, learning often starts as a social experience before becoming something they do individually inside their minds. Helping students understand their worth, build positive connections with others, and establish healthy boundaries in their relationships lays crucial groundwork for their academic success and overall personal development.

This *Relationships and Belonging* curriculum is designed for students in **2nd through 9th grade** and offers 10 interactive 30-minute lessons that aim to cultivate social awareness, helping students understand their own emotions, perspectives, and how their behavior impacts others. Increased social awareness is the foundation for developing crucial interpersonal skills needed to build and maintain positive, healthy relationships. By learning to recognize social cues and understand diverse viewpoints, students will enhance their ability to connect with peers and teachers, thereby improving their overall learning experience. The lessons are designed to be adaptable, ensuring that each student can actively participate, grasp these key personal growth concepts, and practice the skills necessary for building strong relationships.

The strategic design allows students to connect with others and translate their new knowledge into practice. The American School Counselor Association (ASCA®)-aligned curriculum contains an introductory lesson, ten core lessons, and a final closing lesson. Facilitators can include the introductory and final chapters as part of the core sessions if they have extra time.

You'll find a range of essential resources in the book's concluding pages. These consist of permission and completion letters, attendance logs, a group expectation form, and a certificate of completion. You'll also find pre- and post-group surveys to measure the success of the programming and templates you may use to share the results with interested parties. Moreover, this workbook provides a comprehensive small group action plan that integrates seamlessly into your ASCA evaluation documents, facilitating a smooth transition from planning to assessment.

Practical and applicable, the activities are suitable for small or large group instruction and may require a few additional materials. For the most part, you do not need to bring supplies beyond pencils, markers or crayons, and scratch paper. The best part is, you won't need to spend hours prepping materials before meeting with your students because everything you need is included!

See page 108 for information on Downloadable Resources.

What's Included?

Relationships and Belonging offers a comprehensive ten-lesson program and accompanying materials for facilitating group sessions. Following each detailed lesson outline, you'll find practical resources for establishing a small group within your school environment.

Mind Map: An illustrated diagram of cognitive and social development concepts students need for building their sense of Relationships and Belonging. Students should begin each lesson by considering the connection between those concepts and the skills being reviewed.

It is optional to write these, but visuals are helpful for many students. Some have found it beneficial to draw the Mind Map on the board, or you can draw an illustration like a tree with the concept written on the trunk and the related words on the fruit on the tree.

ASCA® Standards: Each lesson includes success criteria for the learning target.

Lesson Introduction: At the start of each lesson, we will introduce a concept and explain it to provide clarity for the upcoming story.

Circle Time Questions: This section includes three questions for the facilitator to use as a starting point for the conversation. These questions enable students to deepen their understanding of the topic and foster a sense of community by discussing and sharing their experiences.

Story Time: Stories related to the concept that should be read aloud to help students understand the ideas being presented.

Coloring Sheets: Allow younger students to visualize the concept. Students can color the sheet while the facilitator shares the initial story or take it home after the lesson is over.

Discussion Questions: Discuss the questions with students to help them process their understanding of the subject.

Skill Practice: Allow students time to practice the skill being presented in the lesson. Be sure to encourage each student to engage in the practice.

Additional Activities: Activities to help students apply the concept in fun and engaging ways.

Closing Considerations: An opportunity to review the concept and ask students to reflect on their new experience with the material.

Would You Rather? Game: Provides an opportunity for students to consider what they would "rather" do related to the lesson's topic. The facilitator can cut out the cards and let students discuss or read aloud while moving from one side of the room to the other to communicate their preferred answer.

Accompanying Group Documents

Action Plan Guide: Provides the necessary information to complete the ASCA® National Model's Small Group Action Plan.

Permission Form: The permission form is used to introduce the Relationships and Belonging group content to the student's caregivers and gain permission for the student to attend the sessions. Be sure to send this home about two weeks before the group starts.

Group Expectations: These provide basic expectations for the group process. The form has space for the facilitator and the group to collaborate on adding additional expectations tailored to their specific group needs.

Group Attendance Form: This blank form allows the facilitator to track which students attended each session and what topics were discussed.

Group Attendance Form (Example): This form is an example of how to best utilize the group attendance form.

Mindsets & Behaviors Pre- and Post-Assessment: Provides an opportunity for students to share their understanding of the concepts before and after completing the curriculum.

To measure the progress of students who participate, use the same assessment for both the pre-group and post-group assessments. Administer the pre-group assessment at the start of the instructional period, followed by instruction and practice opportunities for measured skills or knowledge.

At the end of the instructional period, administer the post-group assessment and compare the results of both assessments to identify areas of improvement and areas that need further instruction. Then calculate the average score of the pre-assessment and post-assessment, and determine the percentage of improvement by subtracting the pre-assessment average from the post-assessment average and then dividing the result by the pre-assessment total. Use this pre-assessment average improvement to measure the students' progress effectively.

Percentage of Improvement Formula:
((Post-Assessment Total - Pre- Assessment Total) / Pre- Assessment Total) x 100 = Percentage of Overall Improvement

Example:
(31 Post- Assessment Total - 19 Pre- Assessment Total / 31) x 100 = 63.15% Overall Improvement

Look at your data to determine who should attend your group. Review referrals, attendance data, and achievement metrics to identify students who are experiencing challenges. Consider also tracking students' academic achievements, absences, and discipline referrals. You can better see the impact of your small groups when you strategically select students and closely monitor their academic, attendance, and conduct metrics. Be sure to share the results of your intervention with your advisory council.

Results Report: The Results Report provides a method for sharing your data with interested parties. Remember, we want to ensure that we use graphs and charts because they effectively display our data, which has a greater impact than a paragraph of text. Use the platform of your choice to display your data, but ensure that you complete the data following the group's guidelines, and then share it with interested parties.

Results Report (Example): The Results Report (Example) illustrates what your data might look like after the groups are completed. You can use this form to share your data.

Certificate of Completion: Present to students during the last session and congratulate them on completing the curriculum.

Relationships and Belonging Group Completion Letter: Letter written to the students' caregivers following the completion of the group. Provide to students along with their completion certificates during the last session.

Additional Materials: We promised to provide everything you need in this workbook, and we have. However, you will need to make copies of the pre- and post-assessments, and print the Coloring Sheets and applicable worksheets. You might also print and cut the "Would You Rather?" game, facilitate that activity verbally, or use technology to incorporate an online version of the game. We recommend having crayons, markers, or colored pencils readily available for the "Color Your Mood" check-in activity and for those who wish to complete the Coloring Sheet. It might also be helpful to have some **fidget tools or other sensory items** accessible for your students during their group session.

Other Optional Materials:

- "Color Your Mood" Check-in Activity - chart paper, poster board, or butcher paper
- Chapter 3 Additional Activity – yarn or heavy string
- Chapter 6 Additional Activity – green and red paper, if doing the activity seated
- Chapter 10 Additional Activity – bubble solution with bubble wands or bubble machine, hula hoops, or tape

Good luck with your group! I hope your experience is full of meaningful discussions and impactful connections.

Introductory Group Session

Directions & Overview

Conduct this introductory session before starting the regular lessons. This initial meeting will acclimate students to the program's structure, expectations, and foundational tools. They will learn the check-in process utilized in each subsequent session.

Directions: Begin by extending a warm welcome to all participants. Communicate the group's objectives and generate enthusiasm for learning and collaboration.

Assessment: Before proceeding, read the pre-group assessment instructions aloud to the students and have each student complete the form. Carefully examine the completed forms to verify that all questions have been answered.

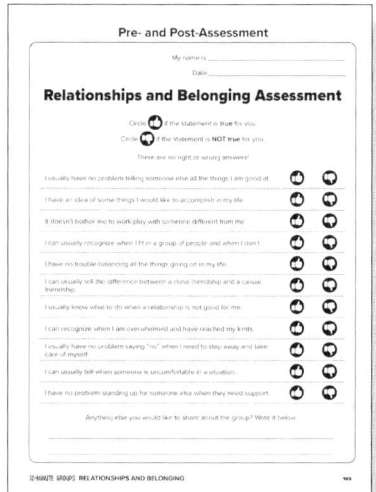

Introductions: Foster a sense of community by encouraging students to share their names, something about themselves, and any thoughts about what it means to "belong." Share with the group that they will be asked to do a "Color Your Mood" check-in at each session. Explain how this works and practice the check-in procedure.

Check-In Activity: Color-Your-Mood Collage

The Color-Your-Mood Collage activity aims to foster empathy and understanding by visually tracking the group's emotional landscape across multiple sessions. Facilitators will bring a large sheet of paper and coloring supplies to each meeting, explaining to participants at the first session that they will choose a color representing their current feeling and then draw a simple, abstract shape on the paper; this process will be repeated at the start of every subsequent session, allowing the collage to grow. Periodically, the facilitator can prompt discussions using the evolving collage, asking questions like "What do you notice about the colors/shapes?" or "How does seeing similar feelings make you feel?" to encourage reflection and connection among participants, who benefit from a non-verbal outlet for expression, a tangible visual of their collective journey, and a low-pressure way to build empathy.

Remind students that not every day is a bright, sunny day, and that's okay. During scheduled group time, be sure to identify a backup person who can be available to assist should a student be unsafe and need immediate attention. Note any student who regularly presents with a depressed affect or expresses extreme emotions, as that may indicate a need to further assess after the session.

Explain the Group Format:

- Explain where and how often you will meet.
- Share the list of topics. Explain that in each meeting, you will discuss one of the topics together, then read the Story and answer questions.

- Discuss the logistics of what they'll do while you are reading the Story; possibly they'll be eating (if it is a lunch group) or completing their Coloring Sheet.
- Explain that they'll have time to work in pairs for the Skill Practice portion, participate in group activities, and play a "Would You Rather?" game.
- Finally, explain that at the end of each session, they'll be asked to give a one-sentence overview of what they've learned and how they plan to practice that lesson topic throughout the week.

Review Group Expectations: Print a copy of the Group Expectations. Review the expectations with the students and answer any questions that arise. Offer students the opportunity to determine whether you need to modify or add expectations.

Group Conclusion: Ask each student to summarize the information they learned from this session into one sentence. Students may share with their partners or the group.

Note to Facilitators: You are encouraged to customize the materials to fit the needs of your group. If your students are not yet strong readers, you can read the "Would You Rather?" game questions aloud and ask students to move to different sides of the room to show their answers. If you're working with reticent students, they can write their responses to questions instead of sharing them aloud, or break into smaller teams. Extension - embed the "Would You Rather?" questions into an online platform and create an electronically interactive game. Some facilitators may wish to incorporate other, more traditional games into the lessons if they have longer session times. Remember, the workbook is a framework that you will bring to life!

30-MINUTE GROUPS: RELATIONSHIPS AND BELONGING

UNDERSTANDING YOUR STRENGTHS

MIND MAP

On the board, draw a Mind Map and ask students to consider the meaning of **Strengths**.

ASCA® STANDARDS

- **B-LS 3.** Time-management, organizational and study skills
- **B-LS 7.** Long- and short-term academic, career and social/emotional goals
- **B-SMS 1.** Responsibility for self and actions
- **B-SMS 8.** Balance of school, home, and community activities

DIRECTIONS

Start with the "Color Your Mood" Check-in activity. Provide crayons or markers and have participants choose a color that represents their feelings today. Participants can use their color to draw a shape on a piece of chart paper. Keep the chart paper visible at each session and watch the collage grow. Use the collage to build empathy by discussing how we share similar emotions and experiences.

Remind students that not every day is a bright, sunny day, and that's okay. During scheduled group time, be sure to identify a backup person who can be available to assist should a student be unsafe and need immediate attention. Note any student who regularly presents with a depressed affect or expresses extreme emotions, as that may indicate a need to further assess after the session.

Review the Group Expectations before reviewing the Mind Map. Then, read the Lesson Introduction and ask the Circle Time Questions before reading the Story and the Discussion Questions. Students can work in pairs to craft their responses or share with the whole group. Complete the Skill Practice, "Would You Rather?" game, and Additional Activities as time allows. Be sure to complete the Closing Considerations with each lesson.

LESSON INTRODUCTION

Understanding who you are begins with recognizing your **strengths** – those things you're naturally good at or have developed skills in. Think about things that come easily to you, or that you feel proud of accomplishing.

Recognizing your **strengths** allows you to contribute positively in friendships and groups. Knowing your **values** guides you in choosing relationships built on mutual respect and shared principles. Reflecting on your life **goals** can help you identify people who support your growth and with whom you can create meaningful connections.

When you understand yourself, you're better equipped to build healthy relationships and find your place within different groups. Let's explore your strengths, values, and goals and how they play a role in your sense of belonging.

CIRCLE TIME QUESTIONS

Ask students to reflect and share their answers to the following questions with the group. Larger groups may need to be broken into smaller groups to give students ample time to share their answers and deepen the conversation.

- What is something you tried that you found you are good at?
- Can you think of a time when you wanted to be good at something, and even though you tried, you just couldn't figure it out?
- How did it make you feel when you tried something, and it went well? What about when you tried something and it didn't go so well?

STORY TIME

Hand out the Coloring Sheets and crayons or markers to younger students while the facilitator reads the story, if desired.

The Treasure Inside You

One day, Mr. Jenkins cleared a space on the classroom whiteboard and wrote: *"The Treasure Inside You"* in big letters. And the class groaned. No one was excited about more writing.

"Today," he said, "we're going on a journey—not across oceans, but into who you are."

"Treasure hunts are for pirates," thought Maya. But then Mr. Jenkins continued, "Think of this like discovering a treasure—your *strengths, values,* and *goals* - buried deep inside you. These are clues to who you are and can guide you to where you truly belong."

Maya wasn't sure what her "strengths" were. She wasn't the best at math, didn't love reading out loud, and wasn't the fastest runner. But as she sat at her desk, she thought about what *did* come easily.

"I'm really good at listening," she wrote. "I can cheer people up when they're upset, and I love organizing group projects so that everyone gets a turn."

As she thought it through, she wrote down her thoughts, and her paper started to fill up.

Later that week, her class was put into teams for a science challenge—to build a bridge out of dry spaghetti and marshmallows. Maya's group had two loud voices trying to take over and one shy student, Evan, who barely said a word.

Normally, Maya would've stayed quiet and let the loud voices win. But today, she remembered one of her strengths—she was good at helping everyone feel included.

"Hey," she said gently, "Evan had an idea earlier. Can we hear it?"

The group paused, surprised, but also interested. Then Evan shared his clever design idea of using triangles for stability. The others nodded, and they gave it a try.

Their bridge held the most weight in the class!

Afterward, Evan pulled Maya aside. "Thanks for speaking up for me," he said quietly.

Maya smiled. "It's one of my strengths," she said, almost laughing. "Turns out, I'm a pretty good team builder."

That night, she added two new sentences to her "treasure map":

I value fairness and kindness.
I want to help others feel seen and heard.

Over time, Maya started to notice how her values helped her choose better friendships—ones where people lifted each other up instead of competing all the time. She realized that it was easier to find people who *"got"* her and helped her feel like she belonged when she understood herself.

And best of all? She didn't need a pirate's map to find treasure—she carried it inside her all along.

DISCUSSION QUESTIONS

- What are some of Maya's strengths? How did she discover them?
- What values did Maya show during the group project?
- How does understanding herself help Maya find "her people?"

SKILL PRACTICE

Strengths, Values, and Goals

Directions: Group students in pairs or groups of three to respond to the prompts below as a team. Explain that one person in the team will be writing their answers on paper or a whiteboard while another person on the team will share their answers with the whole group.

- Think about something you're good at (a **strength**). What did it take to become good at that? How does knowing you are good at this make you feel about yourself?
- What are some things that are important to you – your **values**? Why are these things important *to you*? (Example: Trust - because when people do what they say, I know they won't betray me.)
- Consider a **goal** you have for yourself. What does achieving this goal mean to *you*? What qualities do you have within yourself that will help you reach this goal?

ADDITIONAL ACTIVITIES

Navigating Our Strengths

Directions: Place chairs or tables around the room at odd angles to create a maze-like formation.

Move all students to one side of the room and tell them they are now explorers who must navigate from one side of the room to the other...but with their eyes closed.

As each "explorer" makes it across the room, prompt them to quickly think of one personal strength they used to help them overcome the obstacles and reach the other side. Remind them to think broadly (e.g., creative, problem-solver, persevering, organized, good humor, etc.).

Tip: Write their answers on a whiteboard or have some paper handy, as they may want to write it down, so they don't forget it.

Once everyone has moved through the "maze" to the other side of the room, bring all students to the center of the room to sit/stand in a circle. Go around the circle, allowing each student to state their chosen strength clearly and confidently (e.g., "My strength was that I'm a good problem-solver.").

Immediately after a student shares, the other students in the group are invited to offer a quick, one-word or short-phrase observation of a strength they saw in that person. These are quick flashes of recognition. No need to write anything down.

Example:

- Student A: "My strength was having a good sense of humor even when I banged my shin on the chair."
- Student B: "They're patient!"
- Student C: "They stayed calm."
- Student D: "They were having fun."

Continue to the next student in the circle for their turn to share.

CLOSING CONSIDERATIONS

Today's story showed us that understanding who you are is like a map leading you to discover a treasure inside yourself. When you recognize your **strengths**—the things you're naturally good at or have worked hard to learn—you gain confidence and can use those strengths to help others. Knowing your **values** (things that matter to you) helps you build respectful, meaningful relationships, and having clear **goals** for yourself can guide you toward friendships and other groups that support your growth.

Like Maya in the story, when you take time to explore your strengths, values, and goals, you're better prepared to build healthy relationships and find your place in the world. Everyone has something valuable to offer—and that includes *you*.

Ask students to summarize the content of this session's lesson in one sentence.

"WOULD YOU RATHER?" GAME

Playing the "Would You Rather?" game is a fun and engaging activity for students to develop their critical thinking skills. Students will reflect on their experience, evaluate their options based on their preferences, and reflect on the opinions of others, providing a different perspective and strengthening their sense of connection to one another.

WOULD YOU RATHER?

Copy and cut out the questions for small groups to discuss, or have each person stand in the center of the room and move towards one side or the other to show their vote for either option as the facilitator reads the questions aloud.

- BE GOOD AT SOLVING PROBLEMS OR GOOD AT HELPING OTHERS?

- HAVE THE STRENGTH TO NEVER GIVE UP OR THE COURAGE TO TRY NEW THINGS?

- BE GOOD AT SPORTS OR HAVE ARTISTIC TALENT?

- ALWAYS TELL THE TRUTH OR BE THE BEST AT KEEPING SECRETS?

- MAKE BIG CHANGES ALL AT ONCE OR MAKE SMALL CHANGES THAT TAKE LONGER?

- SET A HARD GOAL THAT'S SUPER EXCITING OR ONE THAT'S EASIER BUT LESS EXCITING?

30-MINUTE GROUPS: RELATIONSHIPS AND BELONGING

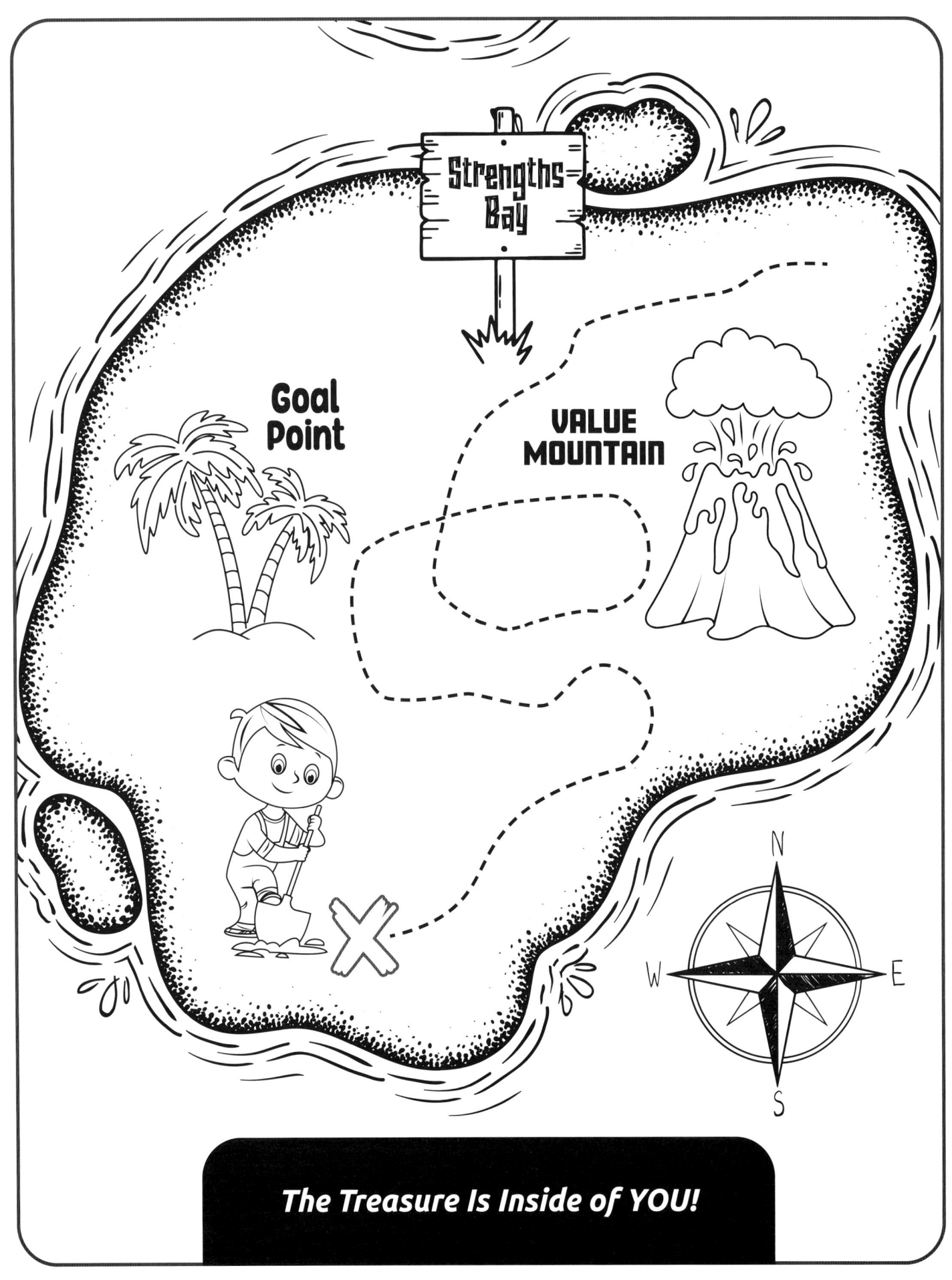

CHAPTER 2
APPRECIATING THE VALUE IN OTHERS

MIND MAP

On the board, draw a Mind Map and ask students to consider the meaning of **Empathy**.

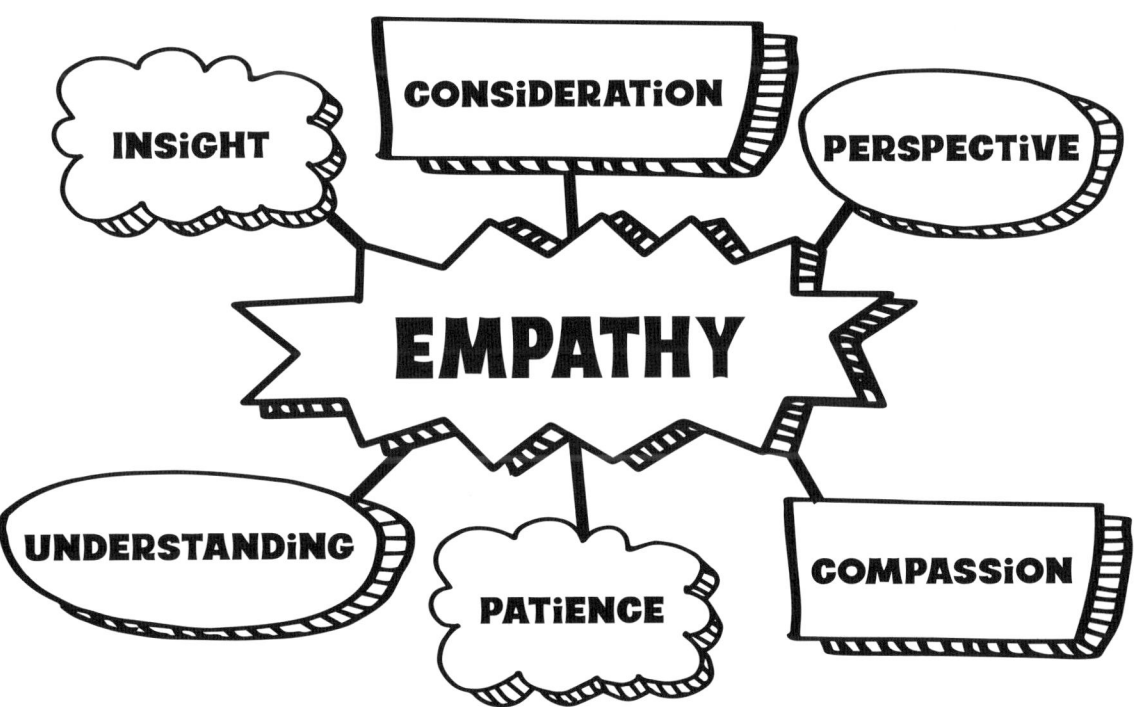

ASCA® STANDARDS

- **B-LS 9.** Decision-making informed by gathering evidence, getting others' perspectives and recognizing personal bias
- **B-SS 4.** Empathy
- **B-SS 2.** Positive, respectful and supportive relationships with students who are similar to and different from them
- **B-SS 7.** Leadership and teamwork skills to work effectively in diverse groups

DIRECTIONS

Start with the "Color Your Mood" Check-in activity. Provide crayons or markers and have participants choose a color that represents their feelings today. Participants can use their color to draw a shape on a piece of chart paper. Keep the chart paper visible at each session and watch the collage grow. Use the collage to build empathy by discussing how we share similar emotions and experiences.

Remind students that not every day is a bright, sunny day, and that's okay. During scheduled group time, be sure to identify a backup person who can be available to assist should a student be unsafe and need immediate attention. Note any student who regularly presents with a depressed affect or expresses extreme emotions, as that may indicate a need to further assess after the session.

Review the Group Expectations before reviewing the Mind Map. Then, read the Lesson Introduction and ask the Circle Time Questions before reading the Story and the Discussion Questions. Students can work in pairs to craft their responses or share with the whole group. Complete the Skill Practice, "Would You Rather?" game, and Additional Activities as time allows. Be sure to complete the Closing Considerations with each lesson.

LESSON INTRODUCTION

Today, let's think about all the different people you meet—each with their personality, opinions, and background. What makes each person special? Understanding these differences and recognizing the value in others helps us build stronger friendships and learn how to work effectively together.

In this session, we'll learn how noticing what you have in common with others—and respecting what's different—can help you create positive and supportive relationships. These skills are important for working and living with all kinds of people.

CIRCLE TIME QUESTIONS

Ask students to reflect and share their answers to the following questions with the group. Larger groups may need to be broken into smaller groups to give students ample time to share their answers and deepen the conversation.

- Is it easier to be around people who are like you or who are different from you?
- Share about a time you met someone new and found out they like the same things you do?
- What does it feel like to get to know someone different from you?

STORY TIME

Hand out the Coloring Sheets and crayons or markers to younger students while the facilitator reads the story, if desired.

The Puzzle Club

Max didn't mean to sign up for Puzzle Club. He thought it was a coding class. But when he walked into Room 204 after school and saw stacks of jigsaw puzzles and a group of kids already digging into boxes, it was too late to back out.

He sighed and sat down at a table with three students he barely knew—Liam, who was always cracking jokes in math; Priya, who never spoke unless called on; and Zahra, a new student from another country who wore a bright scarf and spoke with an accent he had never heard before.

Mr. Salas, the club sponsor, clapped his hands. "Today's challenge: complete the 500-piece puzzle *together*. But here's the twist—no one can touch the puzzle unless everyone in the group agrees on where the piece goes."

Groans filled the room. Max rolled his eyes. "We're never going to finish this."

At first, it was chaos. Liam kept trying to be the leader and talk over everyone. Priya barely looked up. Zahra gently offered ideas, but no one listened. And Max just wanted it to be over.

Then Zahra paused and said, "In my old school, we used to sort edge pieces first. It helped us focus."

The group went quiet. It was a good idea.

"I like that," Priya said softly. "We can make a border first."

Max and Liam exchanged a look. "Okay," Max shrugged. "Let's try it."

As they worked, something shifted. Liam's loud energy actually helped when they got stuck. Priya proved to be amazing at finding the exact piece needed, simply by its shape and color. Zahra had a talent for seeing the big picture and spotting patterns. And Max? He realized he was pretty good at helping the group stay organized and focused.

By the time they finished the puzzle, they were laughing and high-fiving like old friends.

Mr. Salas walked over and smiled. "Looks like you figured out more than just the puzzle."

Later, Max thought about it. They had started off completely different—different personalities, different ways of talking, thinking, and working. But once they listened to each other and respected what each person brought to the table, they became a great team.

And Puzzle Club? Max was already planning to come back next week.

DISCUSSION QUESTIONS

- How were the students in Puzzle Club different from each other?
- What strengths did each student use to complete the puzzle?
- What was Max's attitude toward the Puzzle Club at the beginning? Why do you think he felt differently afterward?

SKILL PRACTICE

Our Similarities and Differences

Directions: Divide students into pairs. Choose a category (i.e., pets, desserts, or flowers). Using the **Similarities and Differences worksheet**, have each pair take three minutes to write down as many similarities as they can think of within that category. Allow the pairs to share what they listed with the whole group.

Using the same category, give the pairs another three minutes to list ways things in that category are different. Allow pairs to share their list of differences with the group.

Optional Extension: If students have access to technology, they can use an online tool to help generate more ideas or create pictures that illustrate similarities and differences.

Reflection: How does noticing similarities help us feel connected to others? How does noticing our differences help us see new ideas or ways of thinking?

ADDITIONAL ACTIVITIES

Stand Up, Speak Up, Switch!

Objective: Encourage students to reflect on real group dynamics, actively practice empathy, and learn how to respect and include others, *all while staying social and moving around the room.*

Directions: Everyone starts by sitting in a circle with one student standing in the middle. The student in the middle reads aloud a peer-to-peer prompt (see below), such as: "Stand up if this has happened to you…" (then finishes the prompt).

All students for whom that prompt applies must stand and switch seats. (There should always be one fewer seat than students, so one student ends up in the middle each time.)

The new person in the middle shares their experience briefly (if they're comfortable doing so) or just reads the next prompt.

Prompts (See a printable version of these **Peer-to-Peer Prompts** later in the chapter):

"Stand up if…"

- You've had an idea ignored in a group project
- You've included someone who looked left out
- You've had to compromise on something you didn't want to
- You've helped a group solve a disagreement
- You've misunderstood someone until you heard their side
- You've stood up for someone who wasn't being treated kindly
- You've been left out of a group decision
- You've had to explain your idea multiple times to be heard
- You've felt proud of how your group worked together
- You've tried to see something from someone else's point of view
- You've been the one to say, "Let's hear from ___, they haven't talked yet."

Reflection: After the activity, give students three minutes to sit with a partner or in a trio and discuss the following questions.

- Did you notice anything you had in common with someone that was unexpected?
- What's one way you can be more understanding next time you work in a group?

CLOSING CONSIDERATIONS

Understanding others means **choosing** to be kind, respectful, and supportive—even when people are different from you. It also means working well in groups by listening to others' ideas and trying to see things from their point of view before making decisions. It's not always easy to stop and listen, but it helps solve problems and maintain strong friendships.

Encourage students to practice these skills next time they work in a group.

Ask students to explain today's lesson in one sentence.

"WOULD YOU RATHER?" GAME

Playing the "Would You Rather?" game is a fun and engaging activity for students to develop their critical thinking skills. Students will reflect on their experience, evaluate their options based on their preferences, and reflect on the opinions of others, providing a different perspective and strengthening their sense of connection to one another.

WOULD YOU RATHER?

Copy and cut out the questions for small groups to discuss, or have each person stand in the center of the room and move towards one side or the other to show their vote for either option as the facilitator reads the questions aloud.

- SPEND A DAY BUILDING LEGOS INSIDE OR MAKING FORTS OUTSIDE?

- HANG OUT WITH ONE GOOD FRIEND WHO "GETS" YOU OR SPEND TIME WITH LOTS OF DIFFERENT FRIENDS ALL AT THE SAME TIME?

- BE INVISIBLE OR BE ABLE TO TELEPORT?

- SPEAK ALL HUMAN LANGUAGES OR SPEAK ALL ANIMAL LANGUAGES?

- LIVE IN SPACE OR LIVE UNDER THE SEA?

- BE FORCED TO SING EVERY TIME YOU TALK OR DANCE EVERY TIME YOU WALK?

30-MINUTE GROUPS: RELATIONSHIPS AND BELONGING

Similarities and Differences

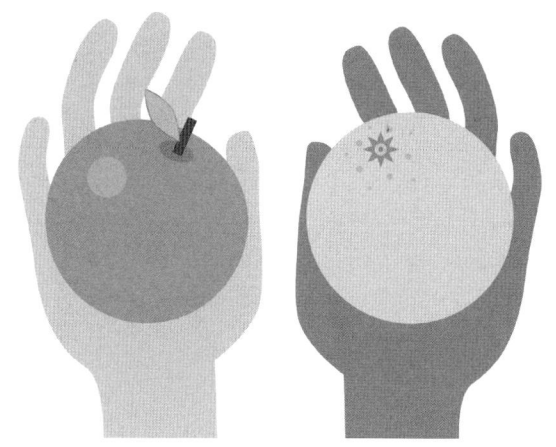

Category: _____

SIMILARITIES	DIFFERENCES

Peer-To-Peer Prompts

Stand up if you've...

had an idea ignored in a group project.

Stand up if you've...

included someone who looked left out.

Stand up if you've...

had to compromise on something you didn't want to.

Stand up if you've...

helped a group solve a disagreement.

Stand up if you've...

misunderstood someone until you heard their side.

Stand up if you've...

stood up for someone who wasn't being treated kindly.

Stand up if you've...

been left out of a group decision.

Stand up if you've...

had to explain your idea multiple times to be heard.

Stand up if you've...

felt proud of how your group worked together.

Stand up if you've...

tried to see something from someone else's point of view.

Stand up if you've...

been the one to say, "Let's hear from ___, they haven't talked yet."

Stand up if you've...

_____
_____

Finding Where You Belong

MIND MAP

On the board, draw a Mind Map and ask students to consider the meaning of **Belonging.**

ASCA® STANDARDS

- **B-LS 10.** Participation in enrichment and extracurricular activities
- **B-SMS 8.** Balance of school, home, and community activities
- **B-SS 9.** Social maturity and behaviors appropriate to the situation and environment

DIRECTIONS

Start with the "Color Your Mood" Check-in activity. Provide crayons or markers and have participants choose a color that represents their feelings today. Participants can use their color to draw a shape on a piece of chart paper. Keep the chart paper visible at each session and watch the collage grow. Use the collage to build empathy by discussing how we share similar emotions and experiences.

Remind students that not every day is a bright, sunny day, and that's okay. During scheduled group time, be sure to identify a backup person who can be available to assist should a student be unsafe and need immediate attention. Note any student who regularly presents with a depressed affect or expresses extreme emotions, as that may indicate a need to further assess after the session.

Review the Group Expectations before reviewing the Mind Map. Then, read the Lesson Introduction and ask the Circle Time Questions before reading the Story and the Discussion Questions. Students can work in pairs to craft their responses or share with the whole group. Complete the Skill Practice, "Would You Rather?" game, and Additional Activities as time allows. Be sure to complete the Closing Considerations with each lesson.

LESSON INTRODUCTION

Have you ever felt like you truly fit in? Like you're exactly where you're supposed to be, surrounded by people who "get" you? That feeling is **belonging**, and it means feeling accepted, valued, and genuinely connected within a group or community. It's a wonderful feeling, and it's something we all want.

Finding where you belong starts with discovering who you are! When you take the time to truly understand your unique **strengths**, **interests**, and core **values**—such as kindness, fairness, or creativity—you begin to discover your authentic self. This self-awareness can guide you in finding your own place to belong.

But belonging isn't just about knowing yourself; it's also about connecting with others. When you learn to genuinely listen to others, to understand their perspectives and what makes them unique, you'll discover shared passions, common values, and new ways to contribute, which will open up opportunities for you to experience meaningful connections.

Finding your place won't always happen instantly, and that's perfectly normal. It takes courage to step outside your comfort zone, try new activities, and meet new people. Sometimes, you might try something and it won't be the right fit - that's absolutely okay! What truly matters is your willingness to keep trying. Every step, every conversation, and every new experience helps you build inner strength and confidence, guiding you closer to the communities and friendships where you can truly feel at home.

CIRCLE TIME QUESTIONS

Ask students to reflect and share their answers to the following questions with the group. Larger groups may need to be broken into smaller groups to give students ample time to share their answers and deepen the conversation.

- Where do you know you belong?
- How do you know you belong there?
- What does it feel like to belong? What does it feel like when you don't belong?

STORY TIME

Hand out the Coloring Sheets and crayons or markers to younger students while the facilitator reads the story, if desired.

Luma

High above the Earth, in the endless expanse of space, a young star named Luma drifted among the constellations. Luma was smaller than most stars and didn't shine as brightly. While others had already formed legendary constellations, Luma felt out of place, always searching for somewhere to belong.

Luma first approached the Big Dipper. "Can I join your constellation?" she asked.

One of the stars flickered kindly. "We admire your glow, Luma, but our shape has been set for centuries. There's no space to fit you in."

Disheartened but not giving up, Luma turned toward Orion's Belt. "Maybe I can be part of your group?"

"You shine beautifully, Luma," Orion's Belt responded, "but we must maintain our perfect line."

Luma drifted away, feeling more lost than ever. Was there anywhere she truly belonged?

For many nights, she orbited alone, questioning if she would always be an outsider. Then, one evening, she noticed a different gathering of stars, their light pulsing excitedly. They were forming something new, and Luma noticed something was missing in their pattern.

"I noticed you have room for one more. I can fill that gap, if that's okay?" Luma bravely asked.

"Yes! Please join us!" said one.

Another said, "We've tried everything and can't seem to find the right fit."

"Every star shines in their special way," another star added, "welcome in!"

Luma felt a new light glow from deep inside her. She took her place among them, and together, they created a stunning new constellation.

As Luma shone in her new home, she realized that belonging wasn't always about fitting in a place that already existed—it was about finding a place where she was needed and valued for who she was. And so, she glowed brighter than ever. Her light is a reminder that there is always a place for everyone, even in the vastness of the universe.

DISCUSSION QUESTIONS

- When Luma was trying to find a place to belong, what did she try first?
- Why did the other constellations reject her?
- What did Luma notice in the new group that gave her the courage to try again?

SKILL PRACTICE

Objective: Help students explore their strengths, interests, and values while practicing the skill of active listening to find points of connection with peers.

Part 1: Discovering My Belonging Blueprint

Directions: Using the *My Strengths, Interests, and Values worksheet*, ask each student to complete the prompts as you read them out:

- **My Strengths**: What am I naturally good at? What do friends or teachers often say I do well?
- **My Interests**: What topics or activities make me feel excited or curious?
- **My Core Values**: What matters most to me? (e.g., kindness, fairness, honesty, fun, helping others)
- **A time I felt like I truly belonged was when...** (Describe where you were, who you were with, and what it felt like.)

Part 2: Partner Listening Exchange

Directions: Divide students into pairs. Have Partner A share **two parts of their blueprint** (e.g., interests and values). Partner B listens silently—no interrupting or reacting.

When A finishes, B reflects back:

- "What I heard you say is..."
- "That reminds me of..."
- "I can relate to that because..."

Switch roles.

Part 3: Group Share and Debrief

Reflection: Use these questions for a group discussion or journaling.

- What did you learn about yourself?
- What surprised you about your partner?
- Did you discover anything in common?
- How can learning more about yourself and others help you find where you belong?

ADDITIONAL ACTIVITIES

We Are Connected

Directions: Sit with the students in a circle. Hand a ball of yarn to a student next to you and ask them to share one thing that interests them (e.g., a hobby, a favorite food, an activity, a subject, etc.).

Any student in the circle who also shares that interest raises their hand.

The student holding the yarn picks one person with their hand raised and tosses the ball of yarn while holding onto the loose end, creating a connection.

The process continues until everyone is connected in a web.

Reflection: When we are connected, we are more likely to feel a sense of belonging. What can you do today to help someone feel connected?

CLOSING CONSIDERATIONS

We feel connected to someone when we share interests, show kindness, or spend time together. It feels good to truly belong. Connection and belonging are important because being part of a group makes us feel safe, happy, and understood.

At times, when we feel left out, we can remind ourselves of our strengths, values, and goals. It's important to seek out groups that accept us for who we are and make us feel valued. At the same time, taking the initiative to help others feel included—by welcoming new people, listening, and showing kindness—can boost our confidence. By fostering a more inclusive and connected environment, we create spaces where everyone feels a sense of belonging.

Ask students to summarize the content of this session's lesson in one sentence.

"WOULD YOU RATHER?" GAME

Playing the "Would You Rather?" game is a fun and engaging activity for students to develop their critical thinking skills. Students will reflect on their experience, evaluate their options based on their preferences, and reflect on the opinions of others, providing a different perspective and strengthening their sense of connection to one another.

Would You Rather?

Copy and cut out the questions for small groups to discuss, or have each person stand in the center of the room and move towards one side or the other to show their vote for either option as the facilitator reads the questions aloud.

- BE ON A SPORTS TEAM OR JOIN AN ART CLUB?

- STAND UP FOR A FRIEND WHO IS LEFT OUT OR INTRODUCE A NEW PERSON TO YOUR FRIENDS?

- BE THE ONE TO PLAN AN EVENT OR BE THE ONE TO HELP SET UP AN EVENT?

- HAVE FRIENDS WHO ALL THINK THE SAME OR HAVE FRIENDS WHO ALL THINK DIFFERENTLY?

- JOIN A GROUP THAT'S ALREADY STARTED A PROJECT OR START A NEW GROUP TO WORK ON A DIFFERENT PROJECT?

- HAVE ONE BEST FRIEND WHO IS JUST LIKE YOU OR A FEW GOOD FRIENDS WITH UNIQUE PERSONALITIES?

30-MINUTE GROUPS: **RELATIONSHIPS AND BELONGING**

My Strengths, Interests, and Values

My Strengths

My Interests

My Core Values

A Time I Felt Like I Truly Belonged Was When...

30-MINUTE GROUPS: **RELATIONSHIPS AND BELONGING**

ACHIEVING WELLNESS AND BALANCE

MIND MAP

On the board, draw a Mind Map and ask students to consider the meaning of **Wellness**.

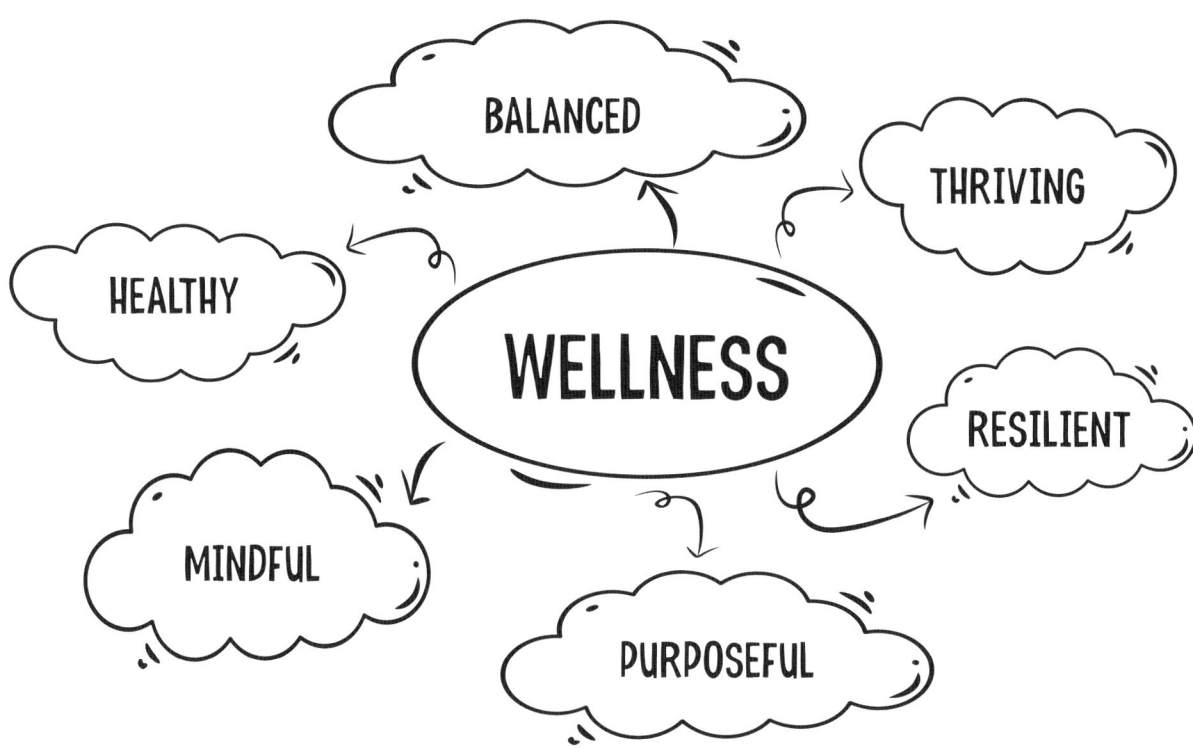

ASCA® STANDARDS

- **B-LS 3.** Time-management, organizational and study skills
- **B-SMS 2.** Self-discipline and self-control
- **B-SMS 8.** Balance of school, home and community activities
- **B-SS 9.** Social maturity and behaviors appropriate to the situation and environment

DIRECTIONS

Start with the "Color Your Mood" Check-in activity. Provide crayons or markers and have participants choose a color that represents their feelings today. Participants can use their color to draw a shape on a piece of chart paper. Keep the chart paper visible at each session and watch the collage grow. Use the collage to build empathy by discussing how we share similar emotions and experiences.

Remind students that not every day is a bright, sunny day, and that's okay. During scheduled group time, be sure to identify a backup person who can be available to assist should a student be unsafe and need immediate attention. Note any student who regularly presents with a depressed affect or expresses extreme emotions, as that may indicate a need to further assess after the session.

Review the Group Expectations before reviewing the Mind Map. Then, read the Lesson Introduction and ask the Circle Time Questions before reading the Story and the Discussion Questions. Students can work in pairs to craft their responses or share with the whole group. Complete the Skill Practice, "Would You Rather?" game, and Additional Activities as time allows. Be sure to complete the Closing Considerations with each lesson.

LESSON INTRODUCTION

Wellness and balance are important because they help you feel good in all parts of your life and in your relationships with others.

- **Physical** wellness involves taking care of your body by eating healthy foods, getting sufficient sleep, and staying physically active. When your body feels strong and healthy, you have more energy to do the things you enjoy.

- **Emotional** wellness involves understanding your emotions and learning how to manage them effectively. Everyone has good days and tough days, but finding ways to stay positive, ask for help, and cope with stress helps you feel happier and more confident.

- **Social** wellness involves feeling connected to friends, family, and your community. Being kind to others, making friends, and finding your place in the world make life more meaningful and enjoyable!

Balance is achieved when you make time for all the various aspects of your life, so that none of them become too overwhelming. If you only focus all your time and energy on one thing—like schoolwork—you might feel stressed or exhausted. But when you balance your time between work and play, rest and exercise, relationships and quiet time alone, you can feel happier and healthier.

Taking care of yourself in these ways helps you perform at your best in school, enjoy your life, and build strength both inside and out.

CIRCLE TIME QUESTIONS

Ask students to reflect and share their answers to the following questions with the group. Larger groups may need to be broken into smaller groups to give students ample time to share their answers and deepen the conversation.

- Share one way you know to stay physically healthy.
- Share one way you know to stay emotionally healthy.
- Share one way you know to stay socially healthy.

STORY TIME

Hand out the Coloring Sheets and crayons or markers to younger students while the facilitator reads the story, if desired.

Emma's Jar of Rocks

Emma was always busy. Between school, cheer practice, piano lessons, science club, and playing with her little sisters, Emma's days were packed. She loved everything she did after school, and she loved her family, but lately she felt tired, stressed out, and like there was never enough time for fun.

One day, her teacher, Mr. Reynolds, noticed Emma rubbing her tired eyes during class. The next morning, he stopped her after class. "Emma, can I share a story with you?" he asked.

Emma shrugged, thinking about what she had to get to next and not wanting to be late. But she was curious, so she nodded and put her backpack down. Mr. Reynolds picked up a jar from his desk and set it on the table. Then, he brought out a tray with some large rocks, small pebbles, and a handful of sand.

"Imagine this jar is your time," he said. "The big rocks are the most important things—your health, family, and well-being. The pebbles are things like school and other activities, and the sand is the little things, like watching TV or playing games."

Emma watched as Mr. Reynolds poured the sand into the jar first. Then he added the pebbles. But when he tried to put in the big rocks, they wouldn't fit.

"Now, let's try again," he said. He dumped everything out on the tray, and this time, he placed the big rocks in first, then the pebbles, and finally the sand. Everything fit perfectly.

Emma's eyes widened. "So, if I focus on the most important things first, I'll still have time for everything else?"

"Exactly," Mr. Reynolds said. "When you take care of your health, rest, and important responsibilities first, the other things will fall into place. But if you let the little things take over, there won't be room for what truly matters."

That night, Emma made a list of her priorities. She decided to get more sleep and schedule breaks between activities. Over the next few weeks, she felt less stressed and began to enjoy the things she was doing after school again. She found that she even had time to watch TV and play more games with her little sisters.

DISCUSSION QUESTIONS

- What did the big rocks, pebbles, and sand represent in Mr. Reynolds' lesson?
- What do you think are the top three most important things ("big rocks") in your life that you should focus on first?
- Mr. Reynolds said your health and rest are some of the most important things. Why do you think it's important to take care of yourself before focusing on smaller, less important tasks?

SKILL PRACTICE

What Would YOU Do?

Using the round-robin method, go around the room and ask students how they would practice each skill, giving everyone a chance to respond. You may want to adapt Skill Practice to allow students to respond in pairs or write out their answers on paper or a whiteboard.

- **Homework vs. Fun** — A student has a big homework assignment due, but also wants to play outside with friends. How can they balance both responsibilities and fun? What would you do?
- **Needing Rest** — A student is staying up late every night to finish schoolwork and is feeling tired and cranky. How can they adjust their schedule to include more rest? What would you do?
- **Too Many Activities** — A student is involved in multiple extracurricular activities, is feeling exhausted, and is struggling to keep up with schoolwork. How can they decide what to prioritize? What would you do?
- **Helping a Friend** — A student notices their friend is always stressed because they are trying to do too much. What advice can they give to help their friend find balance? What would you do?
- **Saying No** — A student is asked to join another club, but they already have a full schedule. How can they politely say no while maintaining friendships and responsibilities? What would you do?

ADDITIONAL ACTIVITIES

Priority Station

Set Up: Establish a "Priority Station" on one side of the room (maybe a desk or a small table). Print and cut out the **Priorities Cards** included so that you have 10 per student. Examples of priorities include:

- School projects/homework
- Sleep
- Family dinner
- Sports team or music practice
- Watching tv
- Playing outside
- Hanging out with friends
- Church or other civic organization
- Watching/creating videos
- Hobby (Legos, knitting, etc.)

Instructions: Divide students into small teams or pairs and send them all to the side of the room opposite the "Priority Station." In a relay, one student from each team must move quickly to the station, pick up a "priority" and bring it back to their teammate(s). The team must decide in what order to place the "priority" (1-10).

Once the "priority" is placed in order, the next teammate quickly moves to the station to retrieve the next slip of paper and bring it back to the team. The teams should keep going one at a time until their priorities are placed in order, 1-10.

Reflection: Once all the teams have completed their priority lists, allow the team that finished first to discuss with the whole group how they chose to distribute their priorities and what they learned about maintaining balance.

CLOSING CONSIDERATIONS

Prioritizing the most important things first can help you feel happier and less stressed. You can make small changes in your daily routine to create a better balance. Taking care of your well-being will help you in school, sports, hobbies, friendships, etc. Together, we can support each other in maintaining balance in our lives.

When you take care of your wellness—your body, your emotions, and your social life—it helps you feel good about yourself, and when you feel good about yourself, it's easier to build relationships where you feel seen, respected, and valued. That's what belonging is all about.

Ask students to summarize the content of this session's lesson in one sentence.

"WOULD YOU RATHER?" GAME

Playing the "Would You Rather?" game is a fun and engaging activity for students to develop their critical thinking skills. Students will reflect on their experience, evaluate their options based on their preferences, and reflect on the opinions of others, providing a different perspective and strengthening their sense of connection to one another.

WOULD YOU RATHER?

Copy and cut out the questions for small groups to discuss, or have each person stand in the center of the room and move towards one side or the other to show their vote for either option as the facilitator reads the questions aloud.

- HAVE ONE HOBBY YOU LOVE OR TRY MANY DIFFERENT ACTIVITIES?

- GET 10 HOURS OF SLEEP EVERY NIGHT BUT HAVE LESS TIME FOR FUN OR GET ONLY FIVE HOURS OF SLEEP BUT HAVE MORE TIME FOR ACTIVITIES?

- SPEND A WEEKEND RELAXING WITH YOUR FAMILY OR GO ON A NEW ADVENTURE WITH FRIENDS?

- ALWAYS BE AHEAD ON YOUR SCHOOLWORK BUT MISS OUT ON SOCIAL TIME OR HAVE LOTS OF SOCIAL TIME BUT ALWAYS FEEL BEHIND AT SCHOOL?

- GIVE UP SCREEN TIME FOR A WEEK TO FOCUS ON WELLNESS OR GIVE UP SWEETS FOR A WEEK TO FOCUS ON HEALTHY EATING?

- EXERCISE EVERY DAY BUT HAVE LITTLE TIME FOR TV OR WATCH TV EVERY DAY BUT HAVE LITTLE TIME FOR EXERCISE?

30-MINUTE GROUPS: RELATIONSHIPS AND BELONGING

Priorities Cards

School Projects/Homework	**Sleep**
Family Dinner	**Sports Team or Music Practices**
Watching TV	**Playing Outside**
Hanging Out with Friends	**Church or Other Civic Organization**
Watching/Creating Videos	**Hobby (Legos, Knitting, Etc.)**

Chapter 5
Defining Healthy Relationships

MIND MAP

On the board, draw a Mind Map and ask students to consider the meaning of **Relationships.**

ASCA® STANDARDS

- **B-SS 2.** Positive, respectful and supportive relationships with students who are similar to and different from them
- **B-SS 8.** Advocacy skills for self and others and ability to assert self, when necessary
- **B-SS 9.** Social maturity and behaviors appropriate to the situation and environment

DIRECTIONS

Start with the "Color Your Mood" Check-in activity. Provide crayons or markers and have participants choose a color that represents their feelings today. Participants can use their color to draw a shape on a piece of chart paper. Keep the chart paper visible at each session and watch the collage grow. Use the collage to build empathy by discussing how we share similar emotions and experiences.

Remind students that not every day is a bright, sunny day, and that's okay. During scheduled group time, be sure to identify a backup person who can be available to assist should a student be unsafe and need immediate attention. Note any student who regularly presents with a depressed affect or expresses extreme emotions, as that may indicate a need to further assess after the session.

Review the Group Expectations before reviewing the Mind Map. Then, read the Lesson Introduction and ask the Circle Time Questions before reading the Story and the Discussion Questions. Students can work in pairs to craft their responses or share with the whole group. Complete the Skill Practice, "Would You Rather?" game, and Additional Activities as time allows. Be sure to complete the Closing Considerations with each lesson.

LESSON INTRODUCTION

In this session, let's talk about something we all care about—**relationships**. That just means the people we're connected to: friends, classmates, family, teammates, even online buddies.

Not every relationship feels the same. Some are **casual**—like someone you say "hi" to in the hallway or chat with during a group project. And some are **close**—like the kind of friend you can laugh with, be yourself around, or tell your secrets to.

So, what makes a relationship feel *real* and *healthy*? Let's break it down: Real and healthy relationships have:

- **Shared Interests** - You don't have to like all the same things, but having stuff in common—like favorite games, music, or sports—makes it easier to connect and have fun together.
- **Kindness** - A real friend treats you kindly, even when they're in a bad mood. They don't make fun of you, talk behind your back, or ignore you when someone "cooler" shows up.
- **Respect** - You listen to each other, don't interrupt just to insert your opinions, and accept your differences. A healthy relationship means no one tries to be the boss all the time.
- **Trust** - You know they won't share your secrets (except to a trusted adult and only to keep you safe) or leave you out on purpose. And you would do the same for them.

CIRCLE TIME QUESTIONS

Ask students to reflect and share their answers to the following questions with the group. Larger groups may need to be broken into smaller groups to give students ample time to share their answers and deepen the conversation.

- What are some ways you include other people in your hobbies?
- How do you show someone you're listening when they talk?
- Tell about a time someone trusted you with something. How did that feel?

STORY TIME

Hand out the Coloring Sheets and crayons or markers to younger students while the facilitator reads the story, if desired.

The Lunch Table Shuffle

It all started on a Monday, right in the middle of mashed potatoes and mystery meat. Jada sat at her usual lunch table with three girls from her art class. They mostly talked about their stuff, and honestly, Jada wasn't even sure if they knew her last name. She just kind of… sat there.

That day, while they were talking about a party Jada wasn't invited to, she glanced across the cafeteria and saw something that made her question her lunch table decision.

At another table, people were laughing—like *really* laughing. Jada spotted Tisha from her English class, who had helped her before during a group project. Tisha had a warm smile and once offered Jada half her cookie just because she "looked like she needed it." Something about that table felt… lighter, warmer. More *real*.

That night, Jada journaled like she always did. She wrote, "**Do I have real friends? Or just people I sit near?**" Then she made a list of what she wanted in a real friend:

- Real friends **ask how you're doing**.
- Real friends **listen**.
- Real friends **make space for you**.
- It's okay to be casual with some people, but I also want a **close friend**.

The next day, she tried something new. When she saw Tisha in the hallway, she said, "Hey, the story you wrote in English yesterday about your cat made me laugh so hard! Do you write a lot?" Tisha blinked, surprised, but smiled. "Yeah! I've got like five unfinished novels. Want to read one?"

Just like that, a door opened. Over the next few weeks, Jada took little steps.

- She invited Tisha to draw at the park one weekend.
- She messaged an online friend to ask how they were doing instead of just jumping into a game.
- She started texting with a kid from her basketball team—not just about practice times, but life stuff, too.

Not every connection turned into a close friendship. Some stayed casual, and that was fine. But a few started to feel solid and real.

One day, after a movie night at Tisha's house with snacks and silly blanket forts, Tisha said quietly, "I'm glad you started talking to me. You're, like... *a really good friend*."

Jada smiled, warmth buzzing through her like sunlight. "Me too."

And when she passed her old lunch table the next week, she didn't feel left out anymore.

DISCUSSION QUESTIONS

- What did Jada notice was missing in the first group she was sitting with?
- What was different about the group she saw at the other table?
- Do you think it took courage for Jada to make new friends? What did Jada do that was brave?

SKILL PRACTICE

Real Talk, Real Choices

Objective: Provide students with opportunities to apply friendship-building skills in everyday social situations through role-playing and peer discussion. This activity enables them to think critically, share their experiences, and build confidence in using these skills.

Directions: Divide students into groups of 3–4. Give each group a slip of paper with a scenario (see below). Have the students read the scenario and take three minutes to:

- Discuss what's going on
- Identify how the people in the scenario might be feeling
- Decide how they could respond using skills they've learned in the session

Each group **role-plays** or **explains** their response to the class. Classmates can share alternate solutions or give a "thumbs up" for ideas they liked.

Scenarios (See a printable version of the *Real Talk, Real Choices Scenarios* later in the chapter):

- **The Hidden Talent:** You're in art class, and someone brings up singing. You love to sing but have never told anyone because you're afraid they'll judge you. How might you find a way to share that part of yourself?
- **The New Kid:** A new student joins your group for a science project. They seem shy and haven't said much. What could you say or do to help them feel included?
- **Group Project Trouble:** You're working with classmates, and one person keeps interrupting or ignoring another teammate's ideas. How can you step in kindly?
- **No Thanks? Be Kind Anyway:** You helped someone clean up a mess they made, but they didn't bother to say thanks. A few days later you see they need help again. Do you help again? Why or why not?
- **Lunchtime Dilemma:** You see someone sitting alone at lunch—again. You're with your usual group. What could you do today to help them feel noticed or included?

Reflection: What made some situations harder than others? Which skills felt easiest to use? Which felt challenging? What's one skill you want to try using this week in real life?

ADDITIONAL ACTIVITIES

Healthy Relationships Role Play

Directions: Print and cut out the **Relationship Type Cards**. Give one to each student.

- Close Friend
- Teammate
- Online Friend
- Family Member
- Casual Friend

Play music while students walk around the room, avoiding each other. When the music stops, call out a situation from the **scenarios** below. Students will quickly find a partner and discuss how to act out what they would do in that situation based on the relationship "type" they have been given.

Each group gets two to three minutes to quickly discuss and *act out* their mini-scene. Encourage creativity and keep it light – having fun with this is good for students!

Scenarios (See a printable version of these *Healthy Relationships Scenarios* later in the chapter):

- You invited someone to a movie, but they canceled at the last minute. How do you react?
- You're on a team, and someone made a mistake. What do you say?
- Your sibling took something from your room. What do you do?
- A new kid joins your class and doesn't know anyone. What do you do?
- Your friend hasn't responded to you in a few days. How do you react?
- A friend asks for help with homework, but you're busy. What would you say?

After each scene, pause and ask **what type of relationship was that?**

If time allows, rotate cards and repeat for a second round.

CLOSING CONSIDERATIONS

Healthy relationships aren't about being perfect—they're about trying your best to be kind, fair, and open with others. Whether it's your best friend, your cousin, or someone you only talk to online, every connection matters.

Ask students to summarize the content of this session's lesson in one sentence.

"WOULD YOU RATHER?" GAME

Playing the "Would You Rather?" game is a fun and engaging activity for students to develop their critical thinking skills. Students will reflect on their experience, evaluate their options based on their preferences, and reflect on the opinions of others, providing a different perspective and strengthening their sense of connection to one another.

Would You Rather?

Copy and cut out the questions for small groups to discuss, or have each person stand in the center of the room and move towards one side or the other to show their vote for either option as the facilitator reads the questions aloud.

- INCLUDE SOMEONE NEW IN YOUR GROUP OR GO ALONE TO HELP A QUIET CLASSMATE FEEL MORE COMFORTABLE?

- TAKE A BREAK FROM A FRIENDSHIP THAT'S FEELING UNHEALTHY OR TRY TO WORK THINGS OUT?

- PLAY ON A TEAM WITH YOUR BEST FRIEND OR MAKE NEW FRIENDS THROUGH A NEW TEAM?

- TELL A FRIEND THEY HURT YOUR FEELINGS OR STAY QUIET, AND HOPE THINGS GET BETTER?

- HELP A FRIEND WHEN THEY'RE UPSET OR GIVE THEM SPACE AND CHECK IN LATER?

- HANG OUT IN PERSON WITH A FRIEND OR VIDEO CHAT WITH AN ONLINE FRIEND FROM ANOTHER STATE?

30-MINUTE GROUPS: RELATIONSHIPS AND BELONGING

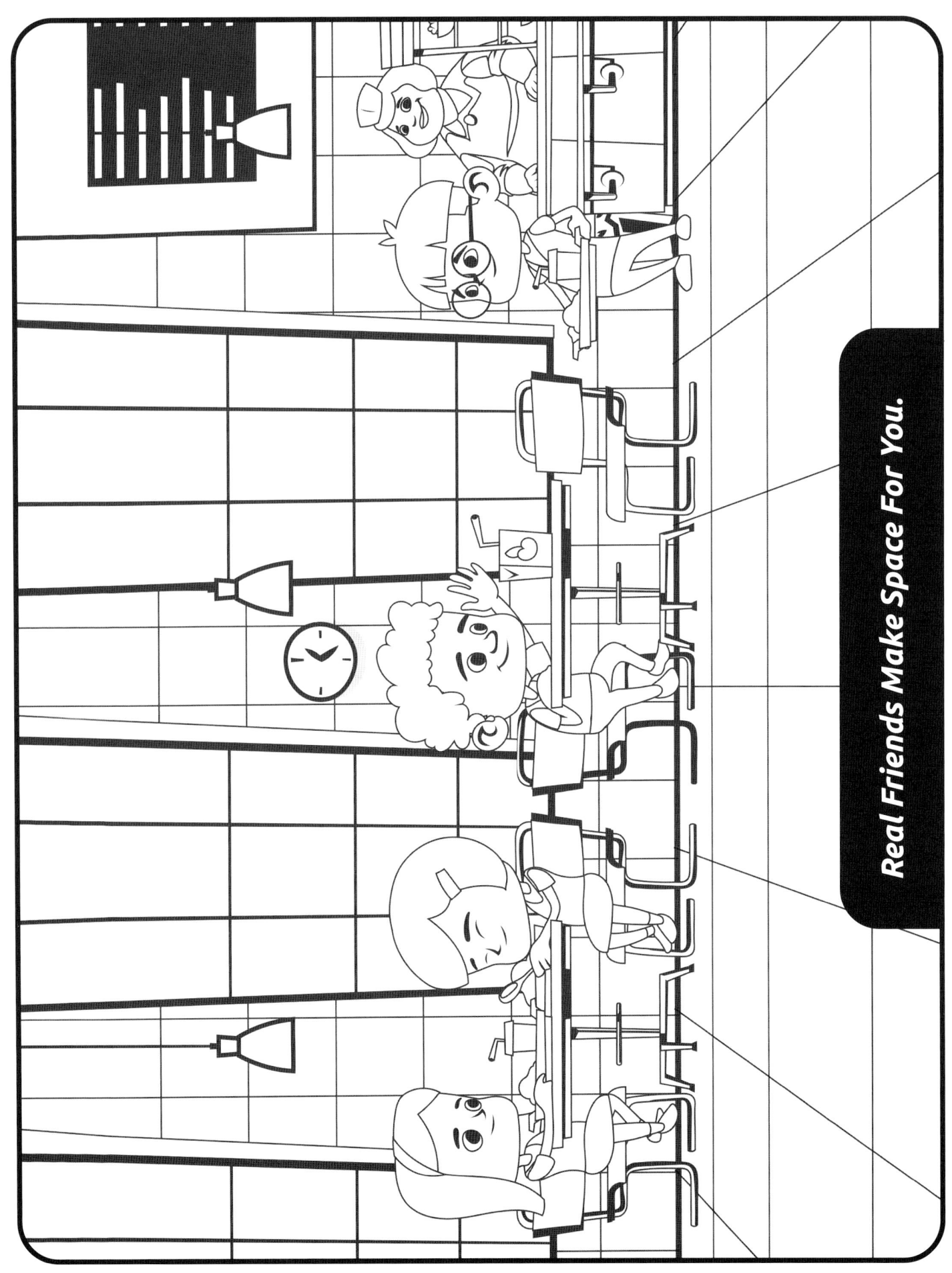

Real Talk, Real Choices Scenarios

The Hidden Talent

You're in art class, and someone brings up singing. You love to sing but have never told anyone because you're afraid they'll judge you. How might you find a way to share that part of yourself?

The New Kid

A new student joins your group for a science project. They seem shy and haven't said much. What could you say or do to help them feel included?

Group Project Trouble

You're working with classmates, and one person keeps interrupting or ignoring another teammate's ideas. How can you step in kindly?

No Thanks? Be Kind Anyway

You helped someone clean up after lunch last week. They didn't say thanks. Now you see them struggling again. Do you help? Why or why not?

Lunchtime Dilemma

You see someone sitting alone at lunch—again. You're with your usual group. What could you do today to help them feel noticed or included?

Relationship Type Cards

Close Friend 	Close Friend 
Teammate 	Teammate 
Online Friend 	Online Friend 
Family Member 	Family Member 
Casual Friend 	Casual Friend 

Healthy Relationships Scenarios

You invited someone to a movie, but they canceled at the last minute. How do you react?

 You're on a team and someone made a mistake. What do you say?

Your sibling took something from your room. What do you do?

 A new student joins your class and doesn't know anyone. What do you do?

Your friend hasn't responded to you in a few days. How do you react?

 A friend asks for help on homework but you're busy. What would you say?

30-MINUTE GROUPS: RELATIONSHIPS AND BELONGING

Recognizing Unhealthy Relationships

MIND MAP

On the board, draw a Mind Map and ask students to consider the meaning of **Toxic**.

ASCA® STANDARDS

- **B-LS 1.** Critical thinking skills to make informed decisions
- **B-LS 2.** Creative approach to learning, tasks and problem solving
- **B-LS 6.** High-quality standards for tasks and activities
- **B-SMS 1.** Responsibility for self and actions
- **B-SMS 6.** Ability to identify and overcome barriers
- **B-SMS 7.** Effective coping skills

DIRECTIONS

Start with the "Color Your Mood" Check-in activity. Provide crayons or markers and have participants choose a color that represents their feelings today. Participants can use their color to draw a shape on a piece of chart paper. Keep the chart paper visible at each session and watch the collage grow. Use the collage to build empathy by discussing how we share similar emotions and experiences.

Remind students that not every day is a bright, sunny day, and that's okay. During scheduled group time, be sure to identify a backup person who can be available to assist should a student be unsafe and need immediate attention. Note any student who regularly presents with a depressed affect or expresses extreme emotions, as that may indicate a need to further assess after the session.

Review the Group Expectations before reviewing the Mind Map. Then, read the Lesson Introduction and ask the Circle Time Questions before reading the Story and the Discussion Questions. Students can work in pairs to craft their responses or share with the whole group. Complete the Skill Practice, "Would You Rather?" game, and Additional Activities as time allows. Be sure to complete the Closing Considerations with each lesson.

LESSON INTRODUCTION

Not all relationships feel good, and it's important to notice that. Sometimes, even people you care about or used to be friends with don't treat you well. You deserve to feel safe, respected, and valued in every relationship you have. If something feels wrong, it's okay to stop, say how you feel, spend less time with that person, or even ask for help from a trusted adult. It's also okay to let some people go. You don't have to keep trying to make a relationship work if it's not good for you.

Let's talk about some things that are *not* healthy in any kind of relationship:

- **Manipulation** - This means someone tries to *control* you or make you feel guilty to get what they want. *Example: "If you were really my friend, you'd give me that."*
- **Dishonesty** - Healthy relationships are built on trust. If someone lies a lot or hides things on purpose, that's a problem.
- **Neglect** - This means someone doesn't make time for you, forgets about you, or stops caring, but still expects you to be there for them.
- **Jealousy** – It's okay to feel left out sometimes, but if someone gets mad at you for having other friends or doing something without them, jealousy can creep in, and that's not healthy.
- **Poor Communication** - If you can never get a word in, or the other person constantly interrupts, ignores, or shuts you down, it's hard to feel safe or heard.
- **Constant Conflict** - Every relationship has its share of small disagreements. But if you're *always* fighting or feeling bad after hanging out with someone, that's not healthy.

CIRCLE TIME QUESTIONS

Ask students to reflect and share their answers to the following questions with the group. Larger groups may need to be broken into smaller groups to give students ample time to share their answers and deepen the conversation.

- You can't control how other people act—but you *can* control how **you** respond. What are some ways to respond to someone treating you poorly in a relationship? (speak up, walk away, set boundaries, etc.)?

- As you grow, your friendships might change. That's normal! What are some things that may happen that can change a relationship (moving away, interests change, new sports teams, etc.)?

- If a relationship becomes toxic, is there someone in your life who is a trusted, safe person you can talk to about it?

STORY TIME

Hand out the Coloring Sheets and crayons or markers to younger students while the facilitator reads the story, if desired.

Lamar's Line

Lamar was 12, fast on the court, and even faster with a comeback. He lived in an apartment near the park where all the neighborhood kids played ball after school. Lamar and his best friend, Jalen, had lived in the same building since they were little. They used to draw sneakers in their notebooks, race to the corner store to buy candy, and talk about growing up to do something big, like, world-changing big.

But things had started to feel different lately.

Jalen started hanging out with some older kids who called themselves "The Crew." They were always posted up near the courts, joking loudly and acting like they ran the place. Lamar noticed that Jalen started dressing like them and talking like them.

One day, Lamar made a nice pass during a game, and after the game, a boy from The Crew called out to him, "Hey - you're fast, kid. You should roll with us. We look out for each other. You don't wanna be left out, right?"

Jalen looked at Lamar and added, "If you're really my boy, you'll come with us. Otherwise, you're soft."

Lamar felt a knot in his stomach and, for once, didn't know what to say. He didn't like how they made fun of other kids. He didn't like the way they tried to act bigger than everyone else. And he *definitely* didn't like how Jalen had started treating him, like Lamar wasn't good enough unless he joined in.

That night, Lamar thought hard. He remembered something his cousin once told him: "You gotta draw a line for yourself. If people make you feel small, that's not a crew—that's control."

So the next day, when Jalen pushed him again to come with The Crew, Lamar stood tall and said, "Nah, I'm not about that. Real friends don't pressure each other to do stuff that feels wrong."

Jalen looked surprised—and a little hurt. But Lamar walked away anyway, heart pounding but head clear.

Later that week, he stayed after school to help with basketball drills for the younger kids. One of the coaches pulled him aside and said, "You got leadership in you, Lamar. Not just skill, but heart too. That matters."

Lamar smiled. He knew he was building something better with his life. It may not be fast, but it was strong.

DISCUSSION QUESTIONS

- Why did Lamar start to feel uncomfortable around Jalen and "The Crew"?
- What were some signs that the relationship between Lamar and Jalen was becoming unhealthy?
- How did Lamar respond when he felt pressured? What do you think about the choice he made?

SKILL PRACTICE

Using the round-robin method, go around the table and ask students to describe how they would practice each skill. Give everyone an opportunity to answer at least one question.

You may want to adapt this Skill Practice to allow students to respond to each other in pairs or put students in groups and ask them to discuss their answers with one another; then have them write their responses on paper or a whiteboard.

Thinking About Real Life

- Have you ever felt pressure to go along with something you didn't feel good about? What did you do?
- What does it mean to "draw a line for yourself"? Why is that important?
- Can you care about someone and still choose to walk away from them? Why or why not?

Healthy vs. Unhealthy Relationships

- What are some ways real friends show respect?
- How can you tell when a friendship is one-sided or unfair?
- Why is it important to notice things like manipulation, dishonesty, or jealousy in a friendship?

Handling Change

- What are some healthy ways to deal with friendships that change over time?
- If you notice a friend is being influenced in a way that's not good for them, what could you do?
- How can you support someone who might be in an unhealthy friendship or pressured by others?

ADDITIONAL ACTIVITIES

Step In or Step Back

Set Up: Prepare an open space that is large enough for everyone to stand in a circle. This is a **movement-based game** where students decide whether a behavior or situation represents a **healthy** or **unhealthy** relationship choice.

Directions: Tell students you will be reading some scenarios. They will be asked to Step In the circle or Step Back out of the circle.

- **"Step In"** if it's a **healthy relationship action** (something they'd want to be part of).
- **"Step Back"** if it's **unhealthy** or makes them uncomfortable (something they'd avoid or question).

Alternative: You can also play seated with **colored cards** (green = Step In, red = Step Back) if space is tight!

Scenarios (See a printable version of these **Step In or Step Back Prompts** later in the chapter):

- **A friend invites you to hang out after school and helps you with your homework.**
  Step In
- **A friend says, "If you don't skip practice with me, we're not cool anymore."**
  Step Back
- **Someone you know makes fun of your new friends.**
  Step Back
- **Your teammate stands up for you when someone tries to embarrass you.**
  Step In
- **A classmate asks you to lie to a teacher for them.**
  Step Back
- **A friend says they miss hanging out and asks if you want to make plans.**
  Step In
- **A group laughs at other kids and tells you to join them so you'll "fit in."**
  Step Back
- **A friend always wants something from you, but disappears when you need help.**
  Step Back
- **You feel safe being yourself around this friend, even when you disagree sometimes.**
  Step In
- **Someone threatens to tell your secret unless you do what they say.**
  Step Back

CLOSING CONSIDERATIONS

Remember this: healthy friendships feel safe, kind, respectful, and honest. It's okay to have boundaries and say "no" if something doesn't feel right. Real friends don't try to control you with guilt or jealousy. The reality is, you can't control how others behave, but you can choose how you act. Friendships can change, and sometimes letting go of one unhealthy relationship makes room for better, healthier ones.

Most importantly, you deserve friends who make you feel good, not bad. Treat others kindly and expect the same in return. Keep making choices that are good for you, even when it's hard. Be the friend you want to have, and spend time with people who share that quality.

Ask students to summarize the content of this session's lesson in one sentence.

"WOULD YOU RATHER?" GAME

Playing the "Would You Rather?" game is a fun and engaging activity for students to develop their critical thinking skills. Students will reflect on their experience, evaluate their options based on their preferences, and reflect on the opinions of others, providing a different perspective and strengthening their sense of connection to one another.

Would You Rather?

Copy and cut out the questions for small groups to discuss, or have each person stand in the center of the room and move towards one side or the other to show their vote for either option as the facilitator reads the questions aloud.

- HAVE ONE HONEST FRIEND WHO ALWAYS HAS YOUR BACK OR FIVE FRIENDS WHO LIE TO MAKE YOU FEEL BETTER?

- SPEAK UP WHEN A FRIEND TREATS YOU UNFAIRLY OR STAY QUIET TO AVOID AN ARGUMENT?

- BE LEFT OUT OF SOMETHING THAT FEELS WRONG OR JOIN IN JUST TO STAY INCLUDED?

- LOSE A FRIEND WHO PRESSURES YOU TO DO THINGS YOU'RE NOT OKAY WITH OR STAY FRIENDS BUT ALWAYS FEEL UNCOMFORTABLE?

- HAVE A FRIEND WHO LISTENS WHEN YOU'RE UPSET OR ONE WHO ONLY TALKS ABOUT THEMSELVES?

- WALK AWAY FROM A FRIENDSHIP THAT FEELS UNHEALTHY OR STAY AND HOPE THINGS CHANGE WITHOUT SAYING ANYTHING?

30-MINUTE GROUPS: RELATIONSHIPS AND BELONGING

Directions: Color in the qualities you want in your circle. Add your own words, symbols, or drawings to show what healthy relationships look like to you. Cross out the things you want to keep out of your circle.

Step In or Step Back Prompts

- **A friend invites you to hang out after school and helps you with your homework.**
  Step In

- **A friend says, "If you don't skip practice with me, we're not cool anymore."**
  Step Back

- **Someone you know makes fun of your new friends.**
  Step Back

- **Your teammate stands up for you when someone tries to embarrass you.**
  Step In

- **A classmate asks you to lie to a teacher for them.**
  Step Back

- **A friend says they miss hanging out and asks if you want to make plans.**
  Step In

- **A group laughs at other kids and tells you to join them so you'll "fit in."**
  Step Back

- **A friend always wants something from you but disappears when you need help.**
  Step Back

- **You feel safe being yourself around this friend, even when you disagree sometimes.**
  Step In

- **Someone threatens to tell your secret unless you do what they say.**
  Step Back

CHAPTER 7
Protecting Your Worth

MIND MAP

On the board, draw a Mind Map and ask students to consider the meaning of **Worthy.**

ASCA® STANDARDS

- **B-LS 1.** Critical thinking skills to make informed decisions
- **B-SMS 1.** Responsibility for self and actions
- **B-SMS 2.** Self-discipline and self-control
- **B-SMS 6.** Ability to identify and overcome barriers
- **B-SMS 9.** Personal safety skills
- **B-SS 2.** Positive, respectful and supportive relationships with students who are similar to and different from them

DIRECTIONS

Start with the "Color Your Mood" Check-in activity. Provide crayons or markers and have participants choose a color that represents their feelings today. Participants can use their color to draw a shape on a piece of chart paper. Keep the chart paper visible at each session and watch the collage grow. Use the collage to build empathy by discussing how we share similar emotions and experiences.

Remind students that not every day is a bright, sunny day, and that's okay. During scheduled group time, be sure to identify a backup person who can be available to assist should a student be unsafe and need immediate attention. Note any student who regularly presents with a depressed affect or expresses extreme emotions, as that may indicate a need to further assess after the session.

Review the Group Expectations before reviewing the Mind Map. Then, read the Lesson Introduction and ask the Circle Time Questions before reading the Story and the Discussion Questions. Students can work in pairs to craft their responses or share with the whole group. Complete the Skill Practice, "Would You Rather?" game, and Additional Activities as time allows. Be sure to complete the Closing Considerations with each lesson.

LESSON INTRODUCTION

We've talked about how to develop your strengths and grow by setting goals that match what's important to you. We've also learned how to see the good in people who are different from you, and how that helps you find where you belong. In the last couple of sessions, we discussed what makes a friendship healthy or unhealthy.

Today, we're going to focus on something significant—how to protect your worth in a relationship. That means knowing you deserve to be treated with respect and learning how to stand up for yourself when something doesn't feel right.

You don't have to stay in a friendship that makes you feel small, guilty, or disrespected. You are allowed to speak up. And most of all, you are allowed to protect your worth. In this lesson, we'll discuss how to recognize when something's not right and how to make choices that honor who you are and how you deserve to be treated.

CIRCLE TIME QUESTIONS

Ask students to reflect and share their answers to the following questions with the group. Larger groups may need to be broken into smaller groups to give students ample time to share their answers and deepen the conversation.

- What does it mean to "protect your worth" in a relationship? What might that look like in real life?
- Can a friendship change and still be healthy? How can friends still respect each other as they go their different ways?
- What would you say to a friend who was being treated badly in a friendship?

STORY TIME

Hand out the Coloring Sheets and crayons or markers to younger students while the facilitator reads the story, if desired.

The Group Chat

At first, Ava loved being part of the group chat. It started with a few friends from summer art camp—people who shared memes, funny stories, and thoughts about everything from music to the meaning of life. It felt easy. Real. Like a space where she could just be herself.

But slowly, the vibe shifted.

It started when Brielle added a few of her friends from a different circle. They were quick with comebacks and always had something sarcastic to say. At first, Ava tried to keep up, throwing in jokes, reacting to messages—but something about it didn't sit right.

One night, someone dropped a comment about Ava's playlist: "Of course you'd like that. So on-brand for someone who cries over poetry."

The laughing emojis came fast. Ava stared at the screen, fingers frozen. She felt her stomach twist.

A few days later, another jab—this time about a selfie she posted on her art account. "Didn't know filter overload was your new aesthetic."

No one defended her. In fact, someone added a GIF that made the whole thing worse. Ava didn't respond. Instead, she muted the group and shut off her phone.

That weekend, Ava hung out with Zoe, a friend she had met through a local volunteer group. They painted signs for a community clean-up and ended up talking for hours. Zoe laughed at Ava's nerdy jokes. She asked real questions. She listened.

Later that night, Ava opened the group chat again, scrolling through the messages she'd missed. More sarcasm. More screenshots of people getting mocked. More silence whenever things got uncomfortable.

She took a breath, opened the chat, and typed: "Hey, just want to say I'm stepping back. I've realized this group doesn't make me feel good about myself. No hard feelings, but I'm out."

Then she left the chat.

The silence that followed wasn't scary—it was peaceful. Quiet. She realized something important: real connections aren't about staying included. They're about being *seen* and *valued*.

Over the next few weeks, Ava put more energy into the friendships that felt safe, like Zoe. She joined a virtual art meet-up. She started journaling again. Took long walks without her phone. And bit by bit, she felt stronger.

DISCUSSION QUESTIONS

- Why did Ava start feeling uncomfortable in the group chat?
- What were some signs that the group did not value her as a person?
- When did Ava recognize her worth?
- How did she know it was time to leave the group chat?

SKILL PRACTICE

Stay or Go

Directions: Introduce the activity by saying, *"Sometimes we go through things that feel personal, but we're often not the only ones. Today, we'll explore some experiences many people face in friendships and social situations."*

Pass out a blank piece of paper to each student. Have students write the word **"STAY"** on one side and **"GO"** on the other side. (They can write as big or as small as they'd like and may decorate it if they choose.)

Explain the rules: *"I'll read a statement aloud. If you think the person in the scenario should 'stay' in that relationship, hold up the 'stay' side of your paper. If you think they should 'go,' hold up the 'go' side of your paper. I may invite a few volunteers to share why they chose to 'stay' or 'go'. You may pass at any time."*

Prompts (See a printable version of these **Stay or Go Prompts** later in the chapter):

- I'm in a group that started out fun, but now it feels stressful, and every day I try to find ways to avoid them.
- Someone makes 'jokes' about me that hurt my feelings.
- I've been starting a relationship with someone I like, and they treat me well, but I don't feel like they really know who I am or what I value yet.
- I have a cousin who reminds me that I matter, even when others didn't treat me kindly.
- Some of my friends are doing things that are not safe, and it makes me uncomfortable to be seen with them.
- I've laughed along with a group, even when I didn't think something was funny, just to fit in.
- In my new after-school club, I've felt nervous about being myself because I was afraid of being judged or left out.
- My friend saw someone get left out on purpose, so they asked that person to sit with us at our table.
- I've felt pressure to go along with a group to do some things that I didn't think were safe.
- I had to set a boundary with a friend—even though it was uncomfortable —and they were okay with it.
- I've been told to 'just take a joke' when I was hurt by something someone said.
- One day, when I was having a bad day, my friend asked me to sit with them at lunch.
- My sister told me she was proud of me for standing up for someone else when they were being bullied at the bus stop.
- I've had a friend help me rebuild my confidence after someone made me feel small.
- I've hurt someone's feelings before, but I apologized and they accepted my apology.

ADDITIONAL ACTIVITIES

Superhero to the Rescue

Directions: Print the **Superhero Situation Cards**. Cut out each card and place them on a table/desk on one side of the room.

Split the group into two teams. Each team will send one member at a time to move quickly to the table, pick a scenario, and present a quick solution in their best superhero impression. They then run back and tag the next team member.

The team that successfully completes the relay, with all members coming up with their own unique superhero solution, wins the game. You can give out small prizes or stickers for fun!

Situations (See a printable version of these **Superhero Situation Cards** later in the chapter):

- **Your friend, Alex, is laughing at another student, Max, for wearing glasses. They keep saying, "You look like a nerd."**
  Follow-up: *What would your superhero do to stop the teasing and help Max feel better?*
- **During lunch, you notice that Sarah is sitting by herself. Everyone else is in groups, and no one is talking to her.**
  Follow-up: *What would your superhero do to make Sarah feel included and not lonely?*
- **Your friend, Jamie, is constantly putting down your other friend, Tyler, saying things like, "You'll never be good at sports."**
  Follow-up: *What would your superhero do to help Jamie understand that it's not okay to put others down?*
- **Your classmate, Sam, tells you a secret about feeling bad because they were left out of a group. They're scared of telling anyone because they think others will laugh at them.**
  Follow-up: *What would your superhero do to support Sam and help them feel safe?*
- **You overhear a group of kids making fun of someone's outfit and calling them names behind their back.**
  Follow-up: *What would your superhero do to make sure the bullying stops and that the person who was made fun of feels better?*
- **During a group project, your friend, Mia, is being ignored, and no one listens to her ideas.**
  Follow-up: *What would your superhero do to make sure Mia's voice is heard and respected by everyone?*
- **You're in a group chat, and someone sends a mean message about another student in the class.**
  Follow-up: *What would your superhero do to stop the harmful message and encourage everyone to be kind in the chat?*
- **Your friend, Ryan, is always saying, "It's no big deal," when someone gets hurt or upset. They don't take feelings seriously.**
  Follow-up: *What would your superhero do to help Ryan understand the importance of respecting others' feelings?*
- **A new student, Maya, is trying to join a conversation, but the group ignores her and makes her feel unwelcome.**
  Follow-up: *What would your superhero do to help Maya feel like part of the group and make her feel welcome?*

- **You see two students, Lily and Zoe, arguing. Lily is saying hurtful things, and Zoe looks upset.**
  Follow-up: *What would your superhero do to stop the argument and help Lily and Zoe talk through their problem respectfully?*

CLOSING CONSIDERATIONS

Your worth isn't something anyone else gets to define—it's something you carry with you, no matter what. Real friendships and healthy relationships should make you feel respected, safe, and valued for who you truly are. If someone makes you feel small, guilty, or pressured just to keep the connection, it's okay to set boundaries or walk away. Choosing peace, self-respect, and honesty over popularity or comfort can be tough, but it's one of the strongest things you can do.

Protecting your worth isn't selfish—it's necessary. Because you deserve to be connected in relationships that build you up, not tear you down.

Ask students to summarize the content of this session's lesson in one sentence.

"WOULD YOU RATHER?" GAME

Playing the "Would You Rather?" game is a fun and engaging activity for students to develop their critical thinking skills. Students will reflect on their experience, evaluate their options based on their preferences, and reflect on the opinions of others, providing a different perspective and strengthening their sense of connection to one another.

Would You Rather?

Copy and cut out the questions for small groups to discuss, or have each person stand in the center of the room and move towards one side or the other to show their vote for either option as the facilitator reads the questions aloud.

HAVE A FRIEND WHO ALWAYS TELLS YOU THE TRUTH, EVEN IF IT'S HARD TO HEAR OR A FRIEND WHO ALWAYS SAYS WHAT YOU WANT TO HEAR, EVEN IF IT'S NOT TRUE?

STAND UP FOR SOMEONE WHO IS BEING BULLIED, EVEN IF YOU'RE NERVOUS OR STAY QUIET BECAUSE YOU'RE WORRIED ABOUT WHAT OTHERS WILL THINK?

BE FRIENDS WITH SOMEONE WHO ALWAYS MAKES YOU LAUGH BUT MAKES FUN OF OTHERS OR A FRIEND WHO IS KIND TO EVERYONE, EVEN WHEN THEY'RE FEELING DOWN?

BE PART OF A GROUP OF FRIENDS WHO ALWAYS MAKE YOU FEEL INCLUDED OR A GROUP WHERE YOU SOMETIMES FEEL LEFT OUT, BUT EVERYONE IS NICE TO EACH OTHER?

HELP A FRIEND WHO'S HAVING A TOUGH TIME BUT IS AFRAID TO ASK FOR HELP OR LET THEM FIGURE IT OUT ON THEIR OWN?

FORGIVE A FRIEND WHO ACCIDENTALLY HURT YOUR FEELINGS OR HOLD A GRUDGE AND NOT TALK TO THEM FOR A LONG TIME?

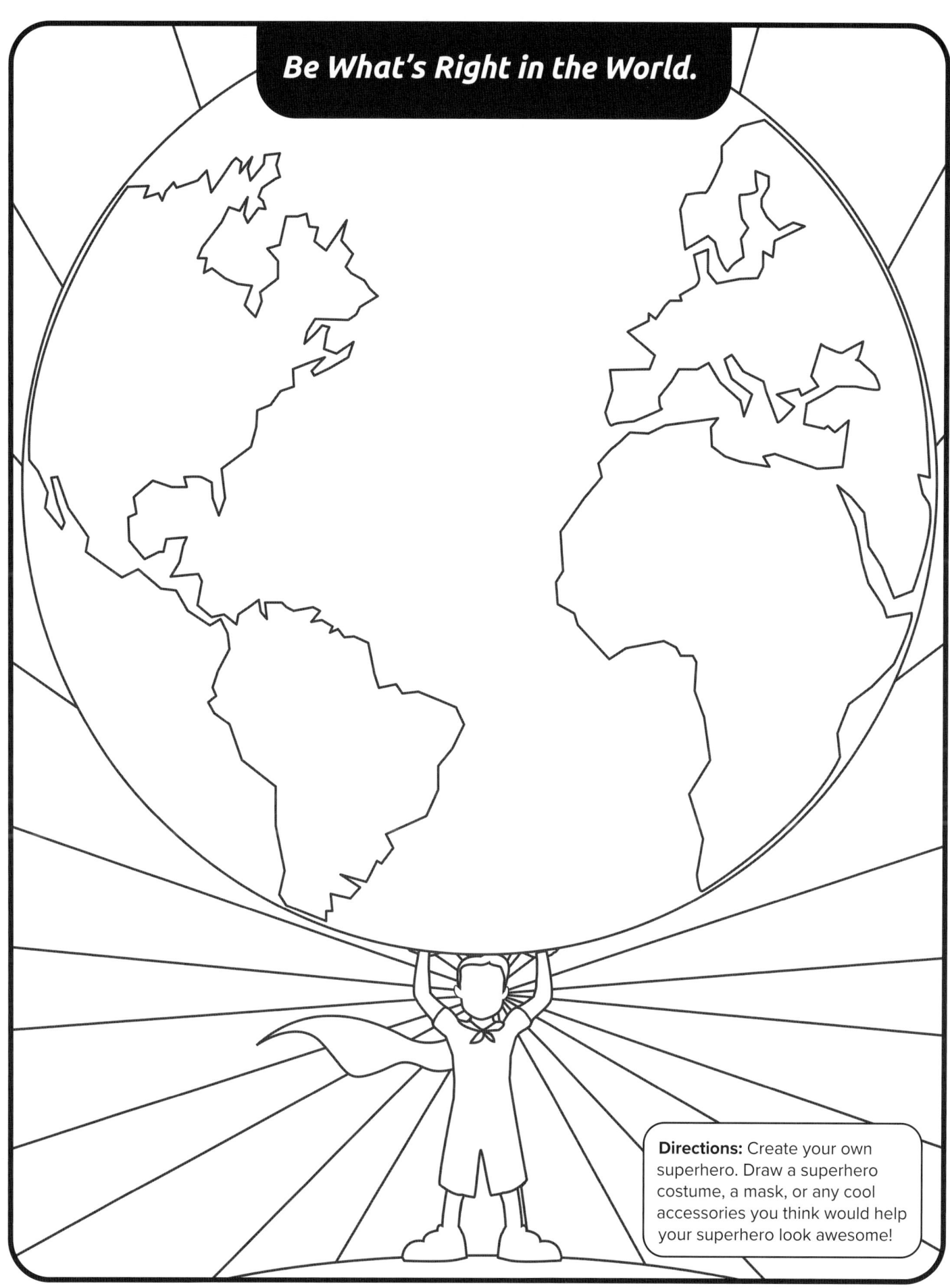

Stay or Go Prompts

- I'm in a group that started out fun, but now it feels stressful and every day I try to find ways to avoid them.
- Someone makes 'jokes' about me that actually hurt my feelings.
- I've been starting a relationship with someone I really like and they treat me well but I don't feel like they really know who I am or what I value yet.
- I have a cousin who reminds me that I matter—even when others didn't treat me kindly.
- Some of my friends are doing things that are really not safe and it makes me uncomfortable to be seen with them.
- I've laughed along with a group, even when I didn't think something was funny—just to fit in.
- In my new after-school club I've felt nervous to be myself because I was afraid of being judged or left out.
- My friend saw someone get left out on purpose so they asked them to come sit with us at our table.
- I've felt pressure to go along with a group to do some things that I didn't think was safe.
- I had to set a boundary with a friend—even though it was uncomfortable, and they were ok with it.
- I've been told to 'just take a joke' when I was hurt by something someone said.
- One day when I was having a bad day, my friend asked me to come sit with them at lunch.
- My sister told me she was proud of myself for standing up for someone else when they were being bullied at the bus stop.
- I've had a friend help me rebuild my confidence after someone made me feel small.
- I've hurt someone's feelings before, but I apologized and they accepted my apology.

Superhero Situation Cards

Your friend, Alex, is laughing at another student, Max, for wearing glasses. They keep saying, "You look like a nerd."

Follow-up: What would your superhero do to stop the teasing and help Max feel better?

During lunch, you notice that Sarah is sitting by herself. Everyone else is in groups, and no one is talking to her.

Follow-up: What would your superhero do to make Sarah feel included and not lonely?

Your friend, Jamie, is constantly putting down your other friend, Tyler, saying things like, "You'll never be good at sports."

Follow-up: What would your superhero do to help Jamie understand that it's not okay to put others down?

Your classmate, Sam, tells you a secret about feeling bad because they were left out of a group. They're scared of telling anyone because they think others will laugh at them.

Follow-up: What would your superhero do to support Sam and help them feel safe?

You overhear a group of kids making fun of someone's outfit and calling them names behind their back.

Follow-up: What would your superhero do to make sure the bullying stops and that the person who was made fun of feels better?

During a group project, your friend, Mia, is being ignored, and no one listens to her ideas.

Follow-up: What would your superhero do to make sure Mia's voice is heard and respected by everyone?

You're in a group chat, and someone sends a mean message about another student in the class.

Follow-up: What would your superhero do to stop the harmful message and encourage everyone to be kind in the chat?

Your friend, Ryan, is always saying, "It's no big deal," when someone gets hurt or upset. They don't take feelings seriously.

Follow-up: What would your superhero do to help Ryan understand the importance of respecting others' feelings?

A new student, Maya, is trying to join a conversation, but the group ignores her and makes her feel unwelcome.

Follow-up: What would your superhero do to help Maya feel like part of the group and welcome her in?

You see two students, Lily and Zoe, arguing. Lily is saying hurtful things, and Zoe looks really upset.

Follow-up: What would your superhero do to stop the argument and help Lily and Zoe talk through their problem respectfully?

CHAPTER 8
DEVELOPING CONSIDERATION FOR OTHERS

MIND MAP

On the board, draw a Mind Map and ask students to consider the meaning of **Consideration.**

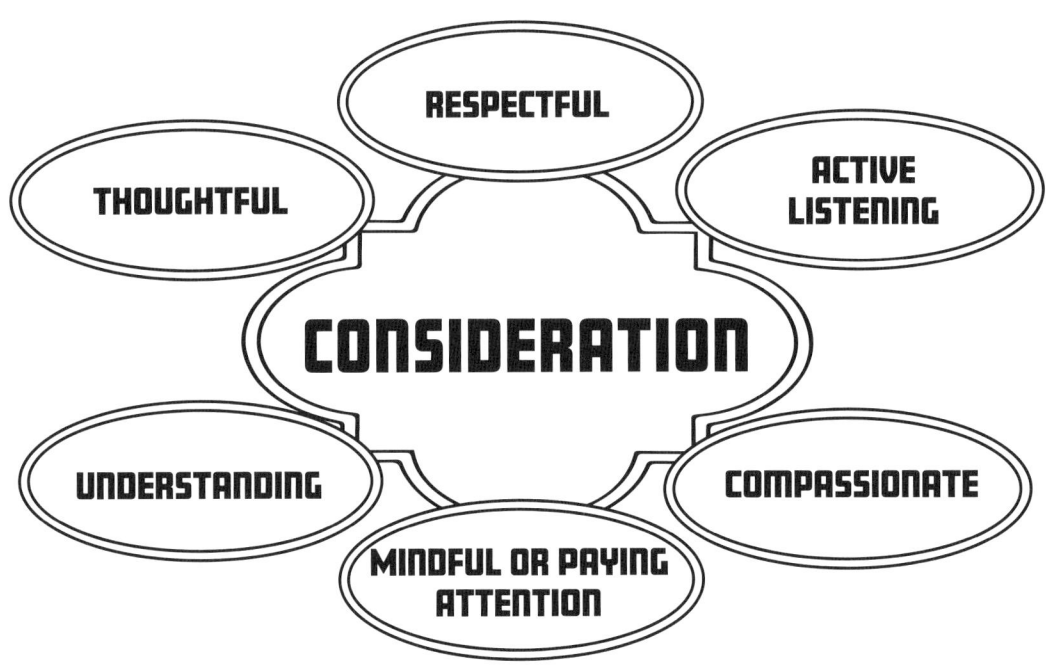

ASCA® STANDARDS

- **B-LS 9.** Decision-making informed by gathering evidence, getting others' perspectives and recognizing personal bias
- **B-SMS 2.** Self-discipline and self-control
- **B-SMS 7.** Effective coping skills
- **B-SMS 9.** Personal safety skills
- **B-SS 2.** Positive, respectful and supportive relationships with students who are similar to and different from them
- **B-SS 3.** Positive relationships with adults to support success
- **B-SS 5.** Ethical decision-making and social responsibility
- **B-SS 8.** Advocacy skills for self and others and ability to assert self, when necessary

DIRECTIONS

Start with the "Color Your Mood" Check-in activity. Provide crayons or markers and have participants choose a color that represents their feelings today. Participants can use their color to draw a shape on a piece of chart paper. Keep the chart paper visible at each session and watch the collage grow. Use the collage to build empathy by discussing how we share similar emotions and experiences.

Remind students that not every day is a bright, sunny day, and that's okay. During scheduled group time, be sure to identify a backup person who can be available to assist should a student be unsafe and need immediate attention. Note any student who regularly presents with a depressed affect or expresses extreme emotions, as that may indicate a need to further assess after the session.

Review the Group Expectations before reviewing the Mind Map. Then, read the Lesson Introduction and ask the Circle Time Questions before reading the Story and the Discussion Questions. Students can work in pairs to craft their responses or share with the whole group. Complete the Skill Practice, "Would You Rather?" game, and Additional Activities as time allows. Be sure to complete the Closing Considerations with each lesson.

LESSON INTRODUCTION

Developing consideration for others means thinking about how other people feel and treating them the way you'd want to be treated. It's about being caring, helpful, and respectful to the people around you. It's more than saying kind things — it's about showing you care through your actions. It can be something small, like sharing your notes with a classmate, or big, like standing up for someone who's being treated unfairly.

Consideration also means paying attention to what others need or want. This is sometimes called being mindful, which involves being present in the moment and noticing if someone looks sad or left out; then putting compassion into action by trying to include them or asking if they're okay.

When you practice being considerate, you help make your school, neighborhood, or community group a happier and safer place for everyone. Plus, it often makes you feel good too!

CIRCLE TIME QUESTIONS

Ask students to reflect and share their answers to the following questions with the group. Larger groups may need to be broken into smaller groups to give students ample time to share their answers and deepen the conversation.

- Why is it important to think about how other people may be feeling before you act or speak?
- How can you tell if someone might need support, even if they don't say anything?
- What challenges might come up when trying to be considerate? What are some ways you could handle those challenges?

STORY TIME

Hand out the Coloring Sheets and crayons or markers to younger students while the facilitator reads the story, if desired.

The Recess Bench

Sixth grade wasn't starting how Jordan had hoped. His best friend had moved away over the summer, and now everything felt... off. He didn't hate school, but it was weird not having someone to talk to during lunch or joke with in the hallway between classes.

One day during recess, Jordan sat alone on the bench by the basketball court, chewing the end of his hoodie string and watching the game. A group of kids were playing, laughing, and calling out plays. Jordan didn't know them well—just faces from class.

Then, one of the players, Malik, missed a shot, and the ball rolled toward the bench. Jordan stood up and grabbed it before it could bounce into the mud.

"Nice save," Malik said, taking the ball back. "You play?"

Jordan shrugged. "A little."

"Cool. Wanna jump in next round?" Malik asked casually.

Jordan hesitated. "Uh, maybe."

Malik didn't pressure him. "All good. I'll holler if we need an extra."

Later, back in class, Malik tapped Jordan's shoulder and asked if he wanted to partner up for a science project. Jordan was surprised—but said yes. Working together turned out to be pretty chill. Malik thoughtfully considered Jordan's ideas and even laughed with him about their cheesy volcano name: "Lava Palooza."

Over the next week, Jordan began to notice little things. Malik would hold the door for the person behind him. He would say "thanks" when someone passed him the scissors. He wasn't trying to be perfect; he just paid attention and treated people like they mattered.

It made Jordan want to do the same.

So when Jordan saw another kid, Leo, sitting by himself at recess the next day, he thought about how it felt to be on that bench. He grabbed a second ball from the rack and jogged over.

"Wanna shoot around?" he asked.

Leo blinked in surprise. "Me?"

"Yeah. Why not?"

As they took turns shooting, Leo smiled more and more. Jordan realized something: Being considerate didn't have to be a big, flashy thing. Sometimes it was as simple as noticing someone who felt invisible—and choosing to make space for them.

DISCUSSION QUESTIONS

- Why do you think Jordan felt uncomfortable at the beginning of the story?
- What was Jordan doing that showed how he was feeling?
- How did Malik show consideration for others without making a big deal out of it?
- What helped Jordan begin to notice and care about others, like Leo?

SKILL PRACTICE

Thumbs Up or Thumbs Down

Directions: Read a statement from the prompts below. Ask students to think about how they feel about it, then show their response with their thumb: Up if they agree, Down if they disagree, or Sideways if they're not sure, or 'it depends'. After each prompt, you may want to call on a volunteer to explain their answer.

Prompts (See a printable version of these *Thumbs Up or Thumbs Down Prompts* later in the chapter):

- **"If I see someone sitting alone, it's my responsibility to help them feel included."**
  Follow-up: *What's one way you could help without making them feel uncomfortable?*
- **"Most people ignore others who are left out because they don't care."**
  Follow-up: *Do you think it's always that simple? What else might be going on?*
- **"Being considerate means doing whatever people ask so they'll like you."**
  Follow-up: *How is kindness different from people-pleasing? Can you say no kindly?*
- **"Saying 'hi' or sharing your supplies with someone can make a big difference."**
  Follow-up: *Why do small actions sometimes matter more than big ones?*
- **"You can be kind to others *and* stand up for yourself at the same time."**
  Follow-up: *How might that look in real life at school?*
- **"It doesn't take much to help make school feel more welcoming."**
  Follow-up: *What's one simple thing anyone could do to help create that vibe?*
- **"Sometimes people are mean because they're having a bad day or feel insecure."**
  Follow-up: *Can understanding that change how we respond to them?*
- **"You should always try to fix someone else's problems for them."**
  Follow-up: *Is supporting someone the same as solving their problems?*
- **"If someone is being picked on, it's better to stay out of it so you don't become a target too."**
  Follow-up: *What are safe ways to speak up or get help instead of staying silent?*
- **"Saying something kind to someone can turn their whole day around."**
  Follow-up: *Has anyone ever said something kind to you that stuck with you?*
- **"Only certain students have the power to make a school feel welcoming."**
  Follow-up: *Who has the power to make school feel better for everyone?*
- **"If someone doesn't fit in with your group, it's okay to ignore them."**
  Follow-up: *What could you do instead that shows inclusion without forcing friendship?*
- **"Helping someone who's struggling is more important than getting all your work done perfectly."**
  Follow-up: *When might helping be more important than perfection? When might it not?*
- **"You can't make a difference unless you do something big."**
  Follow-up: *What's one small action that might be more powerful than it seems?*
- **"Sometimes being kind means standing alone."**
  Follow-up: *What does that mean to you? Have you ever had to do that?*

ADDITIONAL ACTIVITIES

The Heart of Compassion

Set Up: Prepare four stations in the room, one for each of the challenges listed below. For "The Heart of Compassion" station, place blank paper and pencils at this station. You may want to cut the paper into large heart shapes.

Print a copy of **The Heart of Compassion Challenges** and place one challenge at each of the stations. Pair students together and guide them through rotating stations. Give students a hand stamp or sticker as they complete each station.

Challenges:

- **The Listening Wall** Focus: *Active Listening*
  One student shares a simple story (a favorite memory, a pet story, or a fun fact), while the other listens closely. At the end, the listener has to recall three things the speaker said. Switch roles and repeat the activity so that both students have the opportunity to share and practice active listening.
- **The Emotions Mirror** Focus: *Recognizing and responding to feelings*
  One student acts out an emotion (e.g., frustrated, excited, happy). Their partner must guess the emotion and respond with a kind or helpful statement. Switch roles and repeat the activity so that both students have the opportunity to share and practice recognizing and responding to feelings.
- **The Support Bridge** Focus: *Problem-solving with compassion*
  One student shares a made-up challenge ("I lost my book," "I fought with my friend"). The partner role-plays how they would show support. Switch roles and repeat the activity so that both students have the opportunity to share and practice problem-solving with compassion.
- **The Heart of Compassion** Focus: *Reflection and intentional kindness*
  At this station, students will write about one kind thing someone did for them recently and one kind thing they want to do for someone else this week. Ensure each student has the opportunity to reflect on intentional kindness.

After completing all of the challenges, gather the students in a circle and share the "Heart of Compassion" reflections. Remind students that showing consideration for others is a quiet kind of strength. If you have the space, post these hearts in the room where students can see them during future sessions.

Reflection: What is one thing you will do to make your school or friend group feel more welcoming?

CLOSING CONSIDERATIONS

Showing **consideration** for others isn't about always having the right words or never making mistakes. Nobody gets it right all the time—and that's okay. What really counts is *paying attention to the people around you*, noticing how they feel, and choosing to treat them with respect. Being considerate means **thinking about** how your actions might affect others, such as taking the time to include someone who has been left out, or refraining from laughing at a joke that might hurt someone.

These small moments—holding the door, giving a compliment, or saying "thank you"—may seem simple, but they can make a big difference. They let others know: *You matter. I see you.*

And when everyone tries to act with that kind of care, schools and friend groups feel more welcoming. People are more likely to speak up, be themselves, and support each other. That's how you build the kind of friendships where everyone feels safe, valued, and like they belong.

So no, it's not about being perfect. It's about making an effort—trying to be aware, to be respectful, and to treat others the way you'd like to be treated. The more you practice that, the more you'll help create a community that lifts people up instead of tearing them down.

Ask students to summarize the content of this session's lesson in one sentence.

"WOULD YOU RATHER?" GAME

Playing the "Would You Rather?" game is a fun and engaging activity for students to develop their critical thinking skills. Students will reflect on their experience, evaluate their options based on their preferences, and reflect on the opinions of others, providing a different perspective and strengthening their sense of connection to one another.

WOULD YOU RATHER?

Copy and cut out the questions for small groups to discuss, or have each person stand in the center of the room and move towards one side or the other to show their vote for either option as the facilitator reads the questions aloud.

- HELP A LOST CHILD FIND THEIR PARENT OR CHEER UP A FRIEND WHO FEELS LEFT OUT?

- BE THE ONE WHO SOLVES A PROBLEM OR THE ONE WHO LISTENS AND SUPPORTS SOMEONE WHILE THEY SOLVE IT?

- SIT QUIETLY WITH A FRIEND WHO IS SAD OR TRY TO MAKE THEM LAUGH?

- HAVE THE POWER TO FLY ANYWHERE OR THE POWER TO UNDERSTAND WHAT PEOPLE ARE THINKING?

- TALK ABOUT YOUR OWN PROBLEMS OR LISTEN TO SOMEONE TALK ABOUT THEIRS?

- BE KNOWN FOR BEING SUPER BRAVE OR KNOWN FOR BEING SUPER KIND?

30-MINUTE GROUPS: **RELATIONSHIPS AND BELONGING**

Thumbs Up or Thumbs Down Prompts

- "If I see someone sitting alone, it's my responsibility to help them feel included."
  Follow-up: What's one way you could help without making them feel uncomfortable?

- "Most people ignore others who are left out because they don't care."
  Follow-up: Do you think it's always that simple? What else might be going on?

- "Being considerate means doing whatever people ask so they'll like you."
  Follow-up: How is kindness different from people-pleasing? Can you say no kindly?

- "Saying 'hi' or sharing your supplies with someone can actually make a big difference."
  Follow-up: Why do small actions sometimes matter more than big ones?

- "You can be kind to others and stand up for yourself at the same time."
  Follow-up: How might that look in real life at school?

- "It doesn't take much to help make school feel more welcoming."
  Follow-up: What's one simple thing anyone could do to help create that vibe?

- "Sometimes people are mean because they're having a bad day or feel insecure."
  Follow-up: Can understanding that change how we respond to them?

- "You should always try to fix someone else's problems for them."
  Follow-up: Is supporting someone the same as solving their problems?

- "If someone is being picked on, it's better to stay out of it so you don't become a target too."
  Follow-up: What are safe ways to speak up or get help instead of staying silent?

- "Saying something kind to someone can turn their whole day around."
  Follow-up: Has anyone ever said something kind to you that stuck with you?

- "Only certain students have the power to make a school feel welcoming."
  Follow-up: Who really has the power to make school feel better for everyone?

- "If someone doesn't fit in with your group, it's okay to ignore them."
  Follow-up: What could you do instead that shows inclusion without forcing friendship?

- "Helping someone who's struggling is more important than getting all your own work done perfectly."
  Follow-up: When might helping be more important than perfection? When might it not?

- "You can't really make a difference unless you do something big."
  Follow-up: What's one small action that might be more powerful than it seems?

- "Sometimes being kind means standing alone."
  Follow-up: What does that mean to you? Have you ever had to do that?

The Heart of Compassion

The Listening Wall
Focus: Active Listening

One student shares something simple (a favorite memory, pet story, or fun fact), while the other listens closely. At the end, the listener has to recall 3 things the speaker said. Switch roles and do the activity again so that both students have the opportunity to share and to practice active listening.

The Emotions Mirror
Focus: Recognizing and Responding to Feelings

One student acts out an emotion (frustrated, excited, happy, etc.). Their partner must guess the emotion and respond with a kind or helpful statement. Switch roles and do the activity again so that both students have the opportunity to share and to practice recognizing and responding to feelings.

The Support Bridge
Focus: Problem-Solving with Compassion

One student shares a made-up challenge ("I lost my book," "I had a fight with my friend"). The partner role-plays how they would show support. Switch roles and do the activity again so that both students have the opportunity to share and to practice problem-solving with compassion.

The Heart of Compassion
Focus: Reflection and Intentional kindness

At this station students will write one kind thing someone did for them recently, and one kind thing they want to do for someone else this week. Ensure each student has the opportunity to reflect on intentional kindness.

CHAPTER 9

Knowing Your Limits

MIND MAP

On the board, draw a Mind Map and ask students to consider the meaning of **Limits.**

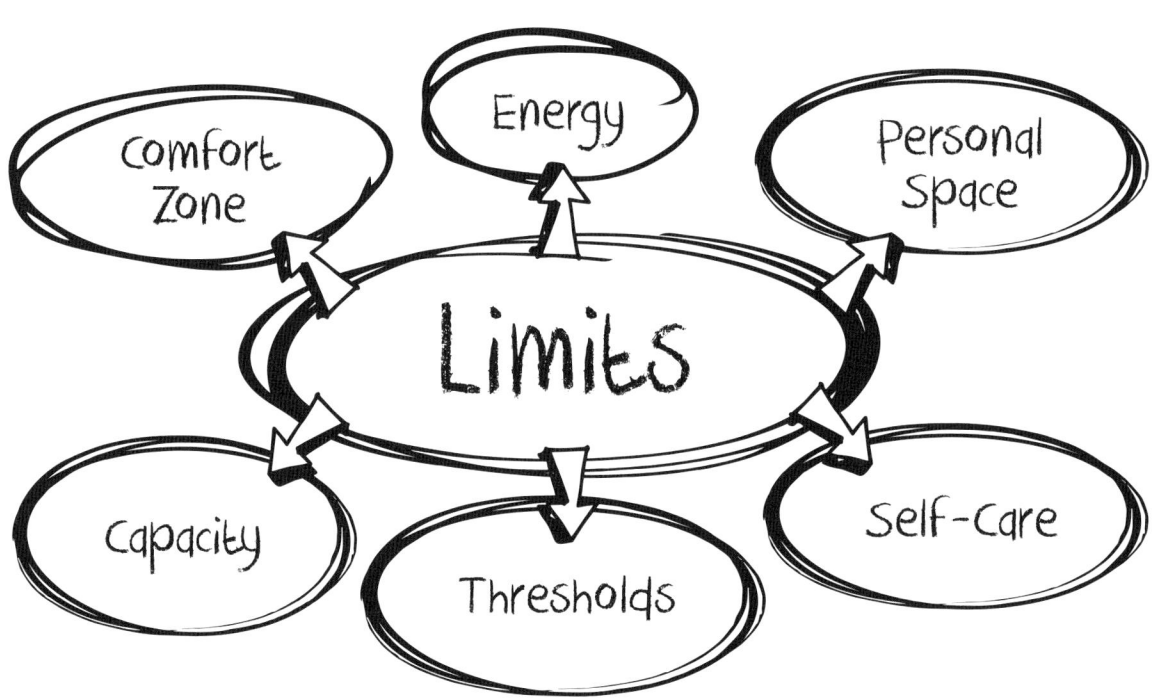

ASCA® STANDARDS

- **B-LS 3.** Time-management, organizational and study skills
- **B-LS 10.** Participation in enrichment and extracurricular activities
- **B-SMS 7.** Effective coping skills
- **B-SMS 8.** Balance of school, home and community activities
- **B-SS 8.** Advocacy skills for self and others and ability to assert self, when necessary
- **B-SS 9.** Social maturity and behaviors appropriate to the situation and environment

DIRECTIONS

Start with the "Color Your Mood" Check-in activity. Provide crayons or markers and have participants choose a color that represents their feelings today. Participants can use their color to draw a shape on a piece of chart paper. Keep the chart paper visible at each session and watch the collage grow. Use the collage to build empathy by discussing how we share similar emotions and experiences.

Remind students that not every day is a bright, sunny day, and that's okay. During scheduled group time, be sure to identify a backup person who can be available to assist should a student be unsafe and need immediate attention. Note any student who regularly presents with a depressed affect or expresses extreme emotions, as that may indicate a need to further assess after the session.

Review the Group Expectations before reviewing the Mind Map. Then, read the Lesson Introduction and ask the Circle Time Questions before reading the Story and the Discussion Questions. Students can work in pairs to craft their responses or share with the whole group. Complete the Skill Practice, "Would You Rather?" game, and Additional Activities as time allows. Be sure to complete the Closing Considerations with each lesson.

LESSON INTRODUCTION

Every person has something called **personal limits**—these are the signals your brain and body send to let you know when you're tired, overwhelmed, uncomfortable, or just need a little space. Perhaps you've had a moment where you felt exhausted but didn't want to let a friend down, got upset but didn't know why, or felt like someone was asking too much of you, but you didn't want to seem rude.

That's where **self-awareness** comes in! Being aware of your energy levels and your own emotional and physical limits enables you to make informed choices in your relationships and daily life.

Setting boundaries isn't mean—it's healthy. It helps you take care of yourself *and* treat others with respect and honesty. By the end of our time today, you'll have tools to understand how to check in with yourself, notice when you need a break or some help, and learn how to say "no" or "not right now" in a respectful way.

Let's dive in and learn how to listen to ourselves so we can connect with others in a strong, safe, and positive way!

CIRCLE TIME QUESTIONS

Ask students to reflect and share their answers to the following questions with the group. Larger groups may need to be broken into smaller groups to give students ample time to share their answers and deepen the conversation.

- Have you ever felt tired or overwhelmed but still tried to help someone? What happened, and how did it make you feel afterward?
- What are some signs your body or mind gives you when you need a break? Examples include getting grumpy, feeling tired, and needing alone time.
- Can you think of a time when you just needed some space, but didn't know how to ask for it? What do you wish you had said or done?

STORY TIME

Hand out the Coloring Sheets and crayons or markers to younger students while the facilitator reads the story, if desired.

Milo's Breaking Point

Milo was always the one people turned to. He helped with the school play, coached the soccer team, organized game days, and was always there when someone needed a hand. He didn't mind—he liked being involved and being the person everyone could count on. It made him feel useful.

But as Game Day got closer, Milo started feeling a little… off. He'd said yes to so many things—helping with the event setup, practicing with friends, organizing the obstacle course—that the hours in his day felt too short. He'd rush from one thing to the next, and before he knew it, it was time to do it all over again.

On Thursday, during lunch, Milo was sitting at his usual spot, his plate was still full, and he wasn't hungry. His mind kept wandering from one thing to the next. He could hear his friends talking and laughing nearby, but it felt like everything was a little… too much. His hands began to shake, and his eyes burned.

Emma sat down next to him, her tray of food in front of her. "Hey, you okay?" she asked, glancing at his untouched lunch.

Milo looked at her and forced a small smile. "Yeah, just thinking about the games."

"Are you sure that's all? You seem quieter than usual." Emma watched him for a moment, waiting for an answer.

Milo hesitated. "I guess… I've just been running around a lot lately."

Emma tilted her head, sensing something wasn't quite right.

Milo said, looking down at his hands. "Just a lot of… little things."

He didn't say anything more. There was a long pause between them, and for a moment, Milo felt the quiet weigh on him. It wasn't uncomfortable, though. Emma didn't push, just sat there with him, letting the silence fill the space.

Finally, Milo looked up. "I'm going to step outside for a bit. Need to get some air."

Emma nodded without asking any more questions. "Take your time."

After a few minutes outside, Milo felt the tension in his chest start to loosen. He wasn't sure what exactly had been bothering him, but he knew he needed a moment to breathe, to let his mind settle. To take a step back and recognize he wasn't ready to give more of himself.

The rest of the afternoon felt lighter. Milo still helped with Game Day setup, but instead of doing it all himself, he asked others to share the work, took breaks when needed, and focused on doing his part well. By slowing down and accepting help, the day felt less rushed and more manageable.

By the end of the day, Milo realized he had set a boundary for himself—not by saying "no" to everything, but by knowing what he could handle and asking for support when things got to be too much. It wasn't just about doing less, but about doing what mattered in a healthier way. And that made all the difference.

DISCUSSION QUESTIONS

- What made Milo feel "heavy" at the beginning of the story?
- Did taking a break fix Milo's problem? What helped him?
- What could you do if you started to feel overwhelmed like Milo?

SKILL PRACTICE

Know and Advocate for Yourself Role Play

Directions: Here are several role-play scenarios using discussion prompts. These scenarios are designed to engage students in practicing skills such as self-awareness and self-advocacy. Each scenario includes a core question and can be facilitated as a group role-play and discussion activity, a pair-share, or a written response.

- **The Overcommitted Friend**
  Prompt: *Have you ever taken on too much? What happened, and what could you do differently next time?*
  Setup: One student pretends to be "Alex," a student who has volunteered for three group projects, offered to tutor a friend, and joined the school play—all in the same week.
  Role Play Task: Students take turns advising Alex. What signs might show Alex has taken on too much? What could Alex do differently next time?

- **The Helpful Teammate**
  Prompt: *Why is it important to recognize your limits, even when you're trying to be helpful?*
  Setup: Two students act out a scenario where "Jamie" wants to help a classmate catch up on missed work, but is also struggling to keep up with their own responsibilities.
  Role Play Task: Each student pair discusses how Jamie might balance helping while recognizing their limits. Then, each student answers the prompt individually.

- **The Group Project Leader**
  Prompt: *How can asking for help be a sign of strength instead of weakness?*
  Setup: A student plays "Taylor," who is leading a group project but is overwhelmed. Taylor is worried that asking for help will make them look weak.
  Role-Play Task: In pairs or small groups, students practice what Taylor could say to their teammates to ask for help respectfully and confidently.

- **The Busy Schedule Warning Signs**
  Prompt: *What are some ways you can tell you might need to set a boundary for yourself?*
  Setup: Students brainstorm signs like feeling tired, irritable, distracted, or falling behind on tasks.
  Role-Play Task: Each student pretends to be someone experiencing these signs and shares the boundary they might need to set (e.g., pretending to be a student with a job who says no to an extra shift, or someone who decides to turn off their phone after 9 pm).

- **Boundaries with Kindness**
  Prompt: *How can setting boundaries help you be kinder to both yourself and others?*
  Setup: Students work in pairs. One plays "Riley," who always says yes, and the other plays a friend asking Riley for a favor.
  Role Play Task: Practice what Riley could say to decline while still being respectful and supportive.

ADDITIONAL ACTIVITIES

Know Your Limits

Directions: Introduce the discussion, *"We all have limits—times when our body or mind is saying 'I need a break,' 'I feel stressed,' or 'I'm exhausted.' Paying attention to those signals helps us take care of ourselves and make smart choices."*

Using the **Know Your Limits worksheet**, have students list ways they can tell when they are reaching their limits on the "What I Notice" side. Examples:

- I get quiet or frustrated
- I can't focus
- My body feels tired
- I feel anxious or annoyed

On the other side, "What I Can Do," have students list helpful responses. Examples:

- Take a few deep breaths
- Ask for a short break
- Talk to someone I trust
- Drink water or stretch

Invite students to share one to two signs and helpful actions with a partner or small group (optional). Remind them it's okay to keep some things private.

Reflection: What is one skill you will practice this week when you notice you are reaching your limit and need to take care of yourself in a healthy, respectful way?

CLOSING CONSIDERATIONS

As we wrap up today, remember this: Everyone has personal limits, and paying attention to them is part of taking care of yourself. Whether you're feeling tired, stressed, or just need a little space, it's okay to notice that and do something about it.

Listening to your own needs helps you make better choices and build stronger, healthier relationships. Communicating that need to others doesn't mean you're being rude—it means you're being honest and respectful to yourself and others.

As you go forward, take a moment to check in with yourself. Ask, "How do I feel?" or "What do I need right now?" It's okay to say "no," ask for help, take a break, or speak up if something feels off. When you do, you're protecting your well-being, which brings balance to your life and in your relationships.

Ask students to summarize the content of this session's lesson in one sentence.

"WOULD YOU RATHER?" GAME

Playing the "Would You Rather?" game is a fun and engaging activity for students to develop their critical thinking skills. Students will reflect on their experience, evaluate their options based on their preferences, and reflect on the opinions of others, providing a different perspective and strengthening their sense of connection to one another.

Would You Rather?

Copy and cut out the questions for small groups to discuss, or have each person stand in the center of the room and move towards one side or the other to show their vote for either option as the facilitator reads the questions aloud.

- POLITELY SAY "NO" WHEN SOMEONE ASKS YOU TO DO SOMETHING YOU'RE NOT COMFORTABLE WITH OR FEEL OVERWHELMED BECAUSE YOU SAID "YES" WHEN YOU SHOULD HAVE SAID "NO"?

- TAKE A BREAK FROM HANGING OUT WITH FRIENDS TO RECHARGE WHEN YOU'RE FEELING TIRED OR KEEP PUSHING YOURSELF TO HANG OUT EVEN THOUGH YOU FEEL DRAINED?

- ASK SOMEONE TO RESPECT YOUR PERSONAL SPACE WHEN YOU NEED IT OR LET THEM KEEP CROSSING YOUR BOUNDARIES BECAUSE YOU DON'T WANT TO UPSET THEM?

- SET A CLEAR BOUNDARY WITH A FRIEND AND MAKE SURE THEY UNDERSTAND YOUR NEEDS OR AVOID SETTING BOUNDARIES AND HOPE THEY FIGURE IT OUT ON THEIR OWN?

- FEEL COMFORTABLE SAYING "NO" WHEN YOU NEED TO, EVEN IF IT'S HARD, OR FEEL STRESSED OUT BY SAYING "YES" TO THINGS YOU DON'T HAVE TIME FOR?

- EXPRESS YOUR FEELINGS OPENLY WITH SOMEONE AND SET BOUNDARIES OR STAY QUIET AND FEEL UNCOMFORTABLE IN SITUATIONS WHERE YOUR LIMITS ARE BEING TESTED?

Make Space to Recharge!

Directions: Color in the things you see that are part of your life.
Fill in the blank stickers with something specific to you.

30-MINUTE GROUPS: RELATIONSHIPS AND BELONGING

Know Your Limits

Under "What I Notice" list ways you can tell you are reaching your limits. Next, list helpful strategies you can use in those situations.

What I Notice	What I Can Do

RESPECTING OTHERS' BOUNDARIES

MIND MAP

On the board, draw a Mind Map and ask students to consider the meaning of **Boundaries**.

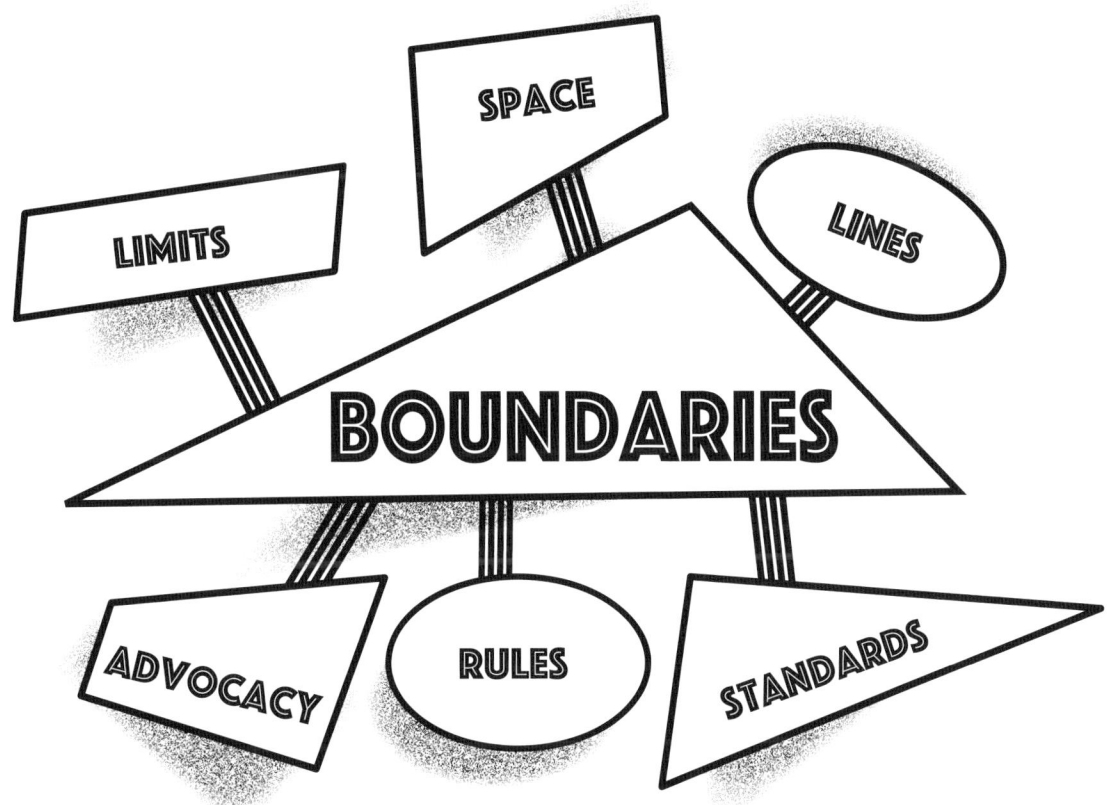

ASCA® STANDARDS

- **B-SMS 1.** Responsibility for self and actions
- **B-SMS 2.** Self-discipline and self-control
- **B-SS 1.** Effective oral and written communication skills and listening skills
- **B-SS 4.** Empathy
- **B-SS 8.** Advocacy skills for self and others and ability to assert self, when necessary
- **B-SS 9.** Social maturity and behaviors appropriate to the situation and environment

DIRECTIONS

Start with the "Color Your Mood" Check-in activity. Provide crayons or markers and have participants choose a color that represents their feelings today. Participants can use their color to draw a shape on a piece of chart paper. Keep the chart paper visible at each session and watch the collage grow. Use the collage to build empathy by discussing how we share similar emotions and experiences.

Remind students that not every day is a bright, sunny day, and that's okay. During scheduled group time, be sure to identify a backup person who can be available to assist should a student be unsafe and need immediate attention. Note any student who regularly presents with a depressed affect or expresses extreme emotions, as that may indicate a need to further assess after the session.

Review the Group Expectations before reviewing the Mind Map. Then, read the Lesson Introduction and ask the Circle Time Questions before reading the Story and the Discussion Questions. Students can work in pairs to craft their responses or share with the whole group. Complete the Skill Practice, "Would You Rather?" game, and Additional Activities as time allows. Be sure to complete the Closing Considerations with each lesson.

LESSON INTRODUCTION

Just like you have feelings, personal limits, and things that make you uncomfortable, other people do too. Respecting someone's boundaries means paying attention to how they feel, listening when they speak up, and not pushing when they ask for space or say "no."

You can't control what other people do, but **you can control your actions**. That means being responsible for how you treat others, whether that's stopping a joke when someone looks uncomfortable, changing the subject, or giving someone space when they need it.

Self-control plays a big role. Even if you want to keep talking or texting, it's important to pause and respect the other person's signals. Doing that shows **maturity** and builds **trust**.

Being respectful also means **communicating clearly and kindly,** as well as being a good listener. Don't just wait for your turn to talk. Pay attention. Try to understand where the other person is coming from. That's **empathy**—seeing the situation from their side and treating them the way you'd want to be treated.

Respecting boundaries doesn't mean you stay quiet when something's wrong. It's okay to speak up for yourself or someone else—just do it in a way that's calm and kind.

And remember, what's okay in one place might not be okay in another. **Social maturity** means knowing how to act in different situations—whether you're at school, online, or hanging out with friends.

Respect is a two-way street. When you honor others' boundaries and stand up for your own, you help create relationships that are healthy, supportive, and real.

CIRCLE TIME QUESTIONS

Ask students to reflect and share their answers to the following questions with the group. Larger groups may need to be broken into smaller groups to give students ample time to share their answers and deepen the conversation.

- What does it mean to respect someone's boundaries?
- Can you think of a time when someone respected your boundary? How did it make you feel?
- Why is it important to listen when someone says "no" or "not right now"?

STORY TIME

If applicable, hand out the Coloring Sheets and crayons or markers while the facilitator reads the story.

Quiet Time at the Lopez House

It was a calm Saturday afternoon at the Lopez house. Carlos, 13, and his sister Mia, 11, usually spent their weekends playing video games, watching movies, or biking around the neighborhood together. They had a close relationship—Carlos was protective of Mia, and she admired her big brother's sense of humor and kindness.

Most days, Mia loved hanging out with Carlos because he made her laugh and always included her in whatever he was doing. Carlos enjoyed having someone to talk to who looked up to him. But sometimes, even the best siblings needed a break from each other.

This Saturday was one of those days. Mia had a tough week at school with a big math test and some misunderstandings with friends. She didn't feel like talking or playing. Instead, she wanted some quiet time alone to relax and recharge.

Carlos noticed something was different about Mia when she didn't join him for an afternoon bike ride. He called out to her, "Mia, come on! Let's go ride bikes."

Mia quietly shook her head and went to her room with a book, closing the door softly behind her.

Just then, Mia's friend Lila showed up at the house, excited to hang out. Lila raced down the hall and banged on Mia's door, "Mia! Let's go outside, it's so nice out! Come on!"

Mia opened her door just a crack, peeked out, and said softly, "Not right now, Lila. I just want some quiet time."

But Lila didn't take the hint. She kept pushing, "You're being weird. We always hang out on Saturdays. Don't be like that."

Mia looked uncomfortable and shut the door gently. Carlos was still outside, so he hadn't noticed the exchange until he came inside and heard Lila pressuring Mia again. This time, Mia sounded upset when she said, "Please go, Lila. I said not right now."

Carlos realized Mia was feeling frustrated. He called out, "Hey Lila, Mia needs some space today."

Lila seemed surprised, but she stepped back and listened as Carlos continued, "I know you want to hang out, but Mia's asking for some quiet time. Let's respect that."

Mia opened the door and gave Carlos a small smile. Lila nodded and said, "Okay, no worries. I get it. Sorry, Mia."

Mia felt relieved when Lila left. Carlos gave her a supportive look and said, "If you want, I'll go outside with Lila and hang out for a little while so you can chill."

Later that evening, Mia came out of her room feeling calmer and more like herself. Carlos was happy to see her smile again and proud that he stood up for her.

Their mom noticed the change, too. She said, "Carlos, you showed real maturity today by standing up for Mia and respecting her needs. Listening and helping others protect their boundaries shows how much you care about your sister."

Carlos realized that sometimes caring means not just giving space but also standing up for someone when they need it. Respecting boundaries helps maintain healthy friendships and strong family relationships.

DISCUSSION QUESTIONS

- Why do you think Lila had trouble respecting Mia's boundary at first?
- How did Carlos notice that Mia was uncomfortable? What did he do to help?
- How can standing up for a friend, like Carlos did for Mia, help make relationships stronger?

SKILL PRACTICE

Pick a Side

Setup: Divide the room by labeling one side "**Side A**" and the other "**Side B**" (or creatively rename them "Respect Rock" and "Boundary Bay" for fun). Read each scenario aloud. Ask students to stand on the side of the room that corresponds to their response.

Prompts and Choices (See a printable version of these *Pick a Side Prompts and Choices* later in the chapter):

- **How can you tell if someone is uncomfortable even if they don't say anything?**
  - **Side A**: You notice their body language (looking away, crossed arms, backing up).
  - **Side B**: You rely on them to say something directly.

  Follow-up: *Can you think of a time when someone didn't speak up, but you knew something was wrong?*

- **Why is it important to respect when someone asks for space or quiet time?**
  - **Side A**: Because everyone deserves to take care of themselves when they're overwhelmed.
  - **Side B**: Because pushing them to talk will help them feel better.

  Follow-up: *How does giving space build trust in a friendship?*

- **What's the best way to help someone who's struggling to say they need space?**
  - **Side A**: Step in and tell the group, "Hey, I think they need a break."
  - **Side B**: Stay near them quietly so they don't feel alone.

  Follow-up: *Are there situations where either choice might be better?*

- Why do you think respecting others' boundaries shows kindness?
  - **Side A**: Because it proves you care about how someone else feels, even if it's different from how you feel.
  - **Side B**: Because it helps the other person avoid drama or pressure.

  Follow-up: *How do you feel when someone respects your boundary without you having to explain it?*

- What can you do if a friend or family member is not respecting someone's boundaries?
  - **Side A**: Speak up and say, "Hey, they asked for space—let's give it to them."
  - **Side B**: Pull them aside later and explain how it looked or felt to others.

  Follow-up: *Which option feels easier to do in the moment? Which feels harder?*

Optional: After each round, choose 2–3 students from each side to explain their thinking. Remind everyone to listen without judging.

ADDITIONAL ACTIVITIES

Personal Space Bubbles

Materials Needed: Bubble solution and bubble wands or a bubble machine, Hula Hoops or tape to create "boundary" lines on the floor.

Setup: Give each student a hula hoop or place tape lines on the floor to indicate where each student's personal space begins and ends. You can either use a bubble machine, blow bubbles yourself, or have students take turns blowing bubbles. The goal is to pop the bubbles without invading other people's space.

Directions: Tell students that they'll be working in teams to "pop" as many bubbles as they can without breaking their personal space boundaries. They'll count how many bubbles they pop as they practice keeping their distance while still working together.

Reflection: How did you stay aware of your space while trying to pop the bubbles? What did you do to help you keep track of your teammate while also trying to stay out of their personal space?

CLOSING CONSIDERATIONS

Respecting others' boundaries is an essential part of growing up and developing social maturity. It means paying attention to how people feel, listening carefully, and giving them the space they need—even if it's different from what you want.

Sometimes, respecting boundaries also means standing up for someone who cannot speak for themselves, just as Carlos did for Mia. When we practice respecting others' boundaries, we develop the courage to build healthy relationships where people feel safe and connected, and can more easily find a place where they belong.

Ask students to summarize the content of this session's lesson in one sentence.

"WOULD YOU RATHER?" GAME

Playing the "Would You Rather?" game is a fun and engaging activity for students to develop their critical thinking skills. Students will reflect on their experience, evaluate their options based on their preferences, and reflect on the opinions of others, providing a different perspective and strengthening their sense of connection to one another.

WOULD YOU RATHER?

Copy and cut out the questions for small groups to discuss, or have each person stand in the center of the room and move towards one side or the other to show their vote for either option as the facilitator reads the questions aloud.

GIVE A FRIEND SPACE WHEN THEY SEEM UPSET OR TRY TO CHEER THEM UP RIGHT AWAY?

STAND UP FOR A FRIEND WHO FEELS UNCOMFORTABLE OR STAY QUIET BECAUSE YOU DON'T WANT TO CAUSE TROUBLE?

SAY "NO" POLITELY WHEN YOU DON'T WANT TO DO SOMETHING OR DO IT ANYWAY JUST TO AVOID HURTING SOMEONE'S FEELINGS?

LISTEN CAREFULLY TO A FRIEND'S PROBLEM OR CHANGE THE SUBJECT TO SOMETHING FUN?

BE HONEST AND RISK HURTING SOMEONE'S FEELINGS OR STAY SILENT AND FEEL UNCOMFORTABLE?

HELP A FRIEND WHO CAN'T STAND UP FOR THEMSELVES OR FOCUS ON YOUR OWN PROBLEMS FIRST?

Respect Others' Boundaries

Draw a bubble around each person without the lines of their bubble touching any other person or their bubble.

Pick-a-Side Prompts and Choices

How can you tell if someone is uncomfortable even if they don't say anything?

- Side A: You notice their body language (looking away, crossed arms, backing up).
- Side B: You rely on them to say something directly.

Follow-up: Can you think of a time when someone didn't speak up, but you knew something was wrong?

Why is it important to respect when someone asks for space or quiet time?

- Side A: Because everyone deserves to take care of themselves when they're overwhelmed.
- Side B: Because pushing them to talk will help them feel better.

Follow-up: How does giving space actually build trust in a friendship?

What's the best way to help someone who's struggling to say they need space?

- Side A: Step in and tell the group, "Hey, I think they need a break."
- Side B: Stay near them quietly so they don't feel alone.

Follow-up: Are there situations where either choice might be better?

Why do you think respecting others' boundaries shows kindness?

- Side A: Because it proves you care about how someone else feels, even if it's different from how you feel.
- Side B: Because it helps the other person avoid drama or pressure.

Follow-up: How do you feel when someone respects your boundary without you having to explain it?

What can you do if a friend or family member is not respecting someone's boundaries?

- Side A: Speak up and say, "Hey, they asked for space—let's give it to them."
- Side B: Pull them aside later and explain how it looked or felt to others.

Follow-up: Which option feels easier to do in the moment? Which feels harder?

Final Group Session

LAST SESSION:
Directions & Overview

This final session is recommended, but optional. You may choose to conclude the group during the final chapter's lesson if time does not permit this final session.

Directions: This final session is designed to be more relaxed and carefree, allowing students to spend time with one another and reflect on their understanding of the group's conclusion. Facilitators may provide structured games or allow students unstructured time together.

Group Check-In: Provide crayons or markers and have the group participants choose a color that represents how they feel today. Allow them to use their color to draw one last shape on the chart paper. Use the collage to build empathy by discussing how we all share similar emotions and experiences. You may want to fill in the blank spaces with a grounding color, laminate it, and post their artwork in a high-traffic area near the group space, where participants will see it regularly and be reminded of the time they spent in these sessions.

Post-Group Expectations: Many students will have grown accustomed to meeting with you and will need reassurance about the support that will be available after the group concludes. Be sure to review the protocol for meeting with you once the group has concluded.

Pre- and Post-Group Assessment: Ask students to complete the Post-Group Assessment. Review the directions aloud. Discreetly ensure that all of the questions were answered when the forms are returned.

Certificate of Completion: Present each student with their Certificate of Completion. You can have as much or as little fanfare around this experience as you would like. Playing a song and asking students to stand and clap for their peers creates lasting memories for the participants.

Group Completion Letter: Distribute the Group Completion Letter to each student to share with their caregiver, notifying them that the group has officially concluded.

Group Conclusion: Ask each student to share what, if anything, this group has meant to them. Model this activity by sharing your experience as the group's facilitator.

Note to Facilitators: If your district permits, concluding a group with a meal can often be a fun experience for the students. If you are unable to purchase a meal with the district budget, perhaps students could bring their lunches. Be sure to obtain caregiver permission and familiarize yourself with the student's allergies before providing them with any food.

ACTION PLAN

GRADE LEVEL
The curriculum is ideal for 2nd through 9th grade students.

GROUP TOPICS
- Understanding Your Strengths
- Appreciating the Value in Others
- Finding Where You Belong
- Achieving Wellness and Balance
- Defining Healthy Relationships
- Recognizing Unhealthy Relationships
- Protecting Your Worth
- Developing Consideration for Others
- Knowing Your Limits
- Respecting Others' Boundaries

10-12 Sessions — 30 MIN

Curriculum:
Use this *Relationships and Belonging* Workbook to facilitate your groups.

Materials:
Copies of the Assessments, Coloring Sheets, Activity Worksheets, and "Would You Rather?" game, crayons or markers, pencils, and scratch paper.

Other Optional Materials:
- "Color Your Mood" Check-in Activity - chart paper, poster board, or butcher paper
- Chapter 3 Additional Activity - yarn or heavy string
- Chapter 6 Additional Activity – green and red paper, if doing the activity seated
- Chapter 10 Additional Activity - bubble solution with bubble wands or bubble machine, hula hoops, or tape

Small group is ideal for up to 6-9 students. Fewer students if the goals are related to behavioral issues.

Relationships and Belonging can be used for classroom lessons.

ASCA® STUDENT BEHAVIOR STANDARDS 21

B-LS 1	B-SMS 1	B-SS 2
B-LS 2	B-SMS 2	B-SS 3
B-LS 3.	B-SMS 6	B-SS 4
B-LS 6	B-SMS 7	B-SS 5
B-LS 7	B-SMS 8	B-SS 7
B-LS 9	B-SMS 9	B-SS 8
B-LS 10	B-SS 1	B-SS 9

ASCA® MINDSETS AND BEHAVIOR DATA

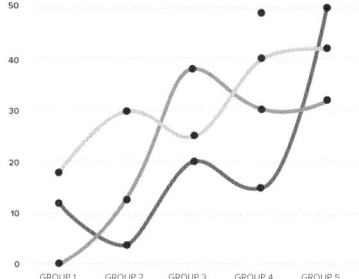

Use the *Relationships and Belonging* pre- and post-assessment data to create a visual representation of their progress, utilizing both their pre- and post-assessment data.

IMPACT DATA

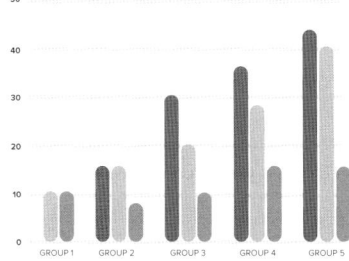

Use achievement, attendance, and discipline data to measure your students' progress. Compare the pre- and post-data to answer the question "how did the learning affect student outcomes?"

RELATIONSHIPS AND BELONGING GROUP PERMISSION FORM

Greetings, Caregivers of: _____,

This form invites your student to attend a **Relationships and Belonging Group**. Our counseling department offers a range of services, including class lessons, small group sessions, and individual counseling sessions with students. Your student is not "in trouble". There are lots of reasons we invite students to attend groups.

Small groups are a fun way for students to learn valuable life skills and connect with their peers. Being part of this group is meant to be a positive experience for all attendees.

We invite students who may need or want support in valuing themselves or others, learning how to create meaningful connections, or setting healthy boundaries. Their involvement will enable them to achieve greater success in their educational and personal journeys.

We will meet for approximately thirty minutes during the school day, ____ times per week. I will work with your child's teacher to select an appropriate time that minimizes interruptions to their learning. When the student has completed all the group sessions, they will receive a Certificate of Completion and will bring home a letter outlining the group's discussions.

I am excited to work with your child. Please don't hesitate to contact me with any questions or concerns.

Warm regards,

_____

-------- ✂ ---

Please complete the form below and return by: _____

Student's Name: _____

Teacher's Name: _____

☐ **YES**, I agree to allow my child to attend the Relationships and Belonging Group.

☐ **I am not sure** if I want my student to attend the Relationships and Belonging Group and need more information before giving my permission.

☐ **NO**, I do NOT agree to allow my child to attend the Relationships and Belonging Group.

_____   _____
Signature of Caregiver   Caregiver Phone Number

RELATIONSHIPS AND BELONGING GROUP EXPECTATIONS

CONFIDENTIALITY

In our group, we will actively listen to each other so that everyone feels respected.

We will keep our discussions confidential. Confidentiality means keeping what is said in the group private and not sharing things we learn about each other outside of the group.

However, because we are an open group in a school setting and cannot promise everything will be kept confidential, we will be mindful of what we share with the group.

SAFETY

We will create an environment of personal safety.
We will not judge or make fun of one another.

It is okay to disagree, but we will not yell at each other or call each other names. Instead, we will ask questions and learn to respect others' opinions.

If anyone shares that they plan to hurt themselves or someone else, or that someone is hurting them, we know it is essential to tell a trusted adult who can help keep them and others safe.

Our group will be a safe place for anyone to ask for and receive help as needed.

BRING OUR BEST

We know that when we open ourselves up to fully participating, we will get more out of the group and grow stronger as individuals.

We will bring our best to the group and actively engage in the discussions and activities.

WE EXPECT

(Here is where we can add to and create our expectations for our group experience.)

_____

_____

Group Attendance Form

Group:_____ Day/Time:_____

	1	2	3	4	5	6	7	8	9	10	11	12
DATE												
	☐	☐	☐	☐	☐	☐	☐	☐	☐	☐	☐	☐
	☐	☐	☐	☐	☐	☐	☐	☐	☐	☐	☐	☐
	☐	☐	☐	☐	☐	☐	☐	☐	☐	☐	☐	☐
	☐	☐	☐	☐	☐	☐	☐	☐	☐	☐	☐	☐
	☐	☐	☐	☐	☐	☐	☐	☐	☐	☐	☐	☐
	☐	☐	☐	☐	☐	☐	☐	☐	☐	☐	☐	☐
	☐	☐	☐	☐	☐	☐	☐	☐	☐	☐	☐	☐

SESSION 1

SESSION 2

SESSION 3

SESSION 4

SESSION 5

SESSION 6

SESSION 7

SESSION 8

SESSION 9

SESSION 10

SESSION 11

SESSION 12

Group Attendance Form (Example)

Group: 5th Grade Lunch **Day/Time:** Thursday@12:30

	1	2	3	4	5	6	7	8	9	10	11	12
DATE	3/2	3/9	3/16	3/23								
Jane/Ms. W's Class	X	X	X	X	X	X	X	X	X	X	X	X
George/Mr. Day's Class	X	X		X	X	X	X	X	X	X	X	X
Sami/Ms. Smith's Class	X	X	X	X	X	X	X	X	X	X	X	X
John/Ms. Lee's Class	X		X	X	X	X	X	X	X	X	X	X
Malik/Ms. Lee's Class	X	X	X		X	X		X	X	X	X	X
Prishna/Ms. Smith's Class	X	X	X	X	X	X	X	X		X	X	X

SESSION 1	Intro/Assessment/Group Rules and Norms/Discussed expectations/Played game.
SESSION 2	Understanding Your Strengths
SESSION 3	Appreciating the Value in Others
SESSION 4	Finding Where You Belong
SESSION 5	Achieving Wellness and Balance
SESSION 6	Defining Healthy Relationships
SESSION 7	Recognizing Unhealthy Relationships
SESSION 8	Protecting Your Worth
SESSION 9	Developing Consideration for Others
SESSION 10	Knowing Your Limits
SESSION 11	Respecting Others' Boundaries
SESSION 12	Check-ins/Assessment/Process group experience & Certificates awarded.

Pre- and Post-Assessment

My name is:_____

Date:_____

Relationships and Belonging Assessment

Circle 👍 if the statement is **true** for you.

Circle 👎 if the statement is **NOT true** for you.

There are no right or wrong answers!

I usually have no problem telling someone else all the things I am good at.	👍	👎
I have an idea of some things I would like to accomplish in my life.	👍	👎
It doesn't bother me to work/play with someone different from me.	👍	👎
I can usually recognize when I fit in a group of people and when I don't.	👍	👎
I have no trouble balancing all the things going on in my life.	👍	👎
I can usually tell the difference between a close friendship and a casual friendship.	👍	👎
I usually know what to do when a relationship is not good for me.	👍	👎
I can recognize when I am overwhelmed and have reached my limits.	👍	👎
I usually have no problem saying "no" when I need to step away and take care of myself.	👍	👎
I can usually tell when someone is uncomfortable in a situation.	👍	👎
I have no problem standing up for someone else when they need support.	👍	👎

Anything else you would like to share about the group? Write it below.

_____

_____

30-MINUTE GROUPS: RELATIONSHIPS AND BELONGING

Results Report
Relationships and Belonging Assessment Data

GROUP GOAL:

STUDENT STATEMENTS:

Academic Results
Increase the total Benchmark scores/Reading Level following group intervention for group participation by ___%

___%

Attendance Results
Decrease the number of absences by ___% following group intervention for group participants

___%

Discipline Results
Decrease the number of conduct referrals by ___% following group intervention

___%

STUDENTS ATTENDED

NUMBER OF SESSIONS

OVERALL IMPROVEMENT

(See Formula Lower Right)

Pre-Assessment % True   Post-Assessment % True

0

- I usually have no problem telling someone else all the things I am good at.
- I have an idea of some things I would like to accomplish in my life.
- It doesn't bother me to work/play with someone different from me.
- I can usually recognize when I fit in a group of people and when I don't.
- I have no trouble balancing all the things going on in my life.
- I can usually tell the difference between a close friendship and a casual friendship.
- I usually know what to do when a relationship is not good for me.
- I can recognize when I am overwhelmed and have reached my limits.
- I usually have no problem saying "no" when I need to step away and take care of myself.
- I can usually tell when someone is uncomfortable in a situation.
- I have no problem standing up for someone else when they need support.

OVERALL IMPROVEMENT FORMULA

$$\left(\frac{\text{Post-Assessment Total} - \text{Pre-Assessment Total}}{\text{Pre-Assessment Total}} \right) \times 100$$

Results Report (Example)
Relationships and Belonging Assessment Data

GROUP GOAL:

Our goal is to help each student gain a deeper understanding of themselves, appreciate the value in others, and foster strong, respectful relationships. We'll learn how to recognize what makes us feel safe, balanced, and valued—both inside ourselves and in our relationships with others.

STUDENT STATEMENTS:

I understand more about myself, and I know how to find healthy relationships where I can belong.

I have learned how to protect my worth while also respecting others.

I know how to stay balanced, recognize what feels right or wrong, and grow in consideration of others, confidence in myself, and connection to my community.

Academic Results
Increase the total Benchmark scores/Reading Level following group intervention for group participation by __5__ %

__5__ %

Attendance Results
Decrease the number of absences by __30__ % following group intervention for group participants

__30__ %

Discipline Results
Decrease the number of conduct referrals by __33__ % following group intervention

__33__ %

STUDENTS ATTENDED: 6

NUMBER OF SESSIONS: 12

OVERALL IMPROVEMENT: 63.15%
(See Formula Lower Right)

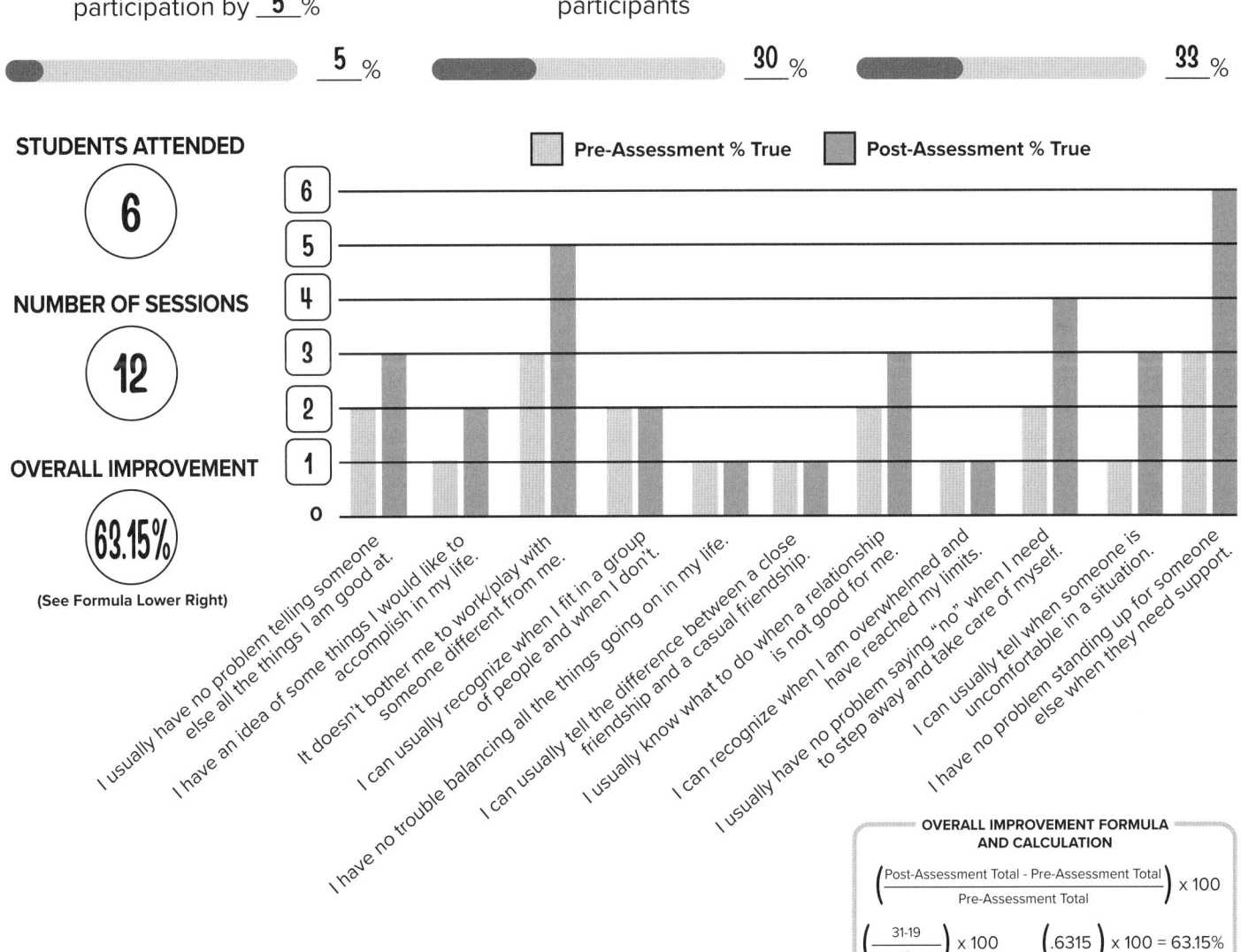

OVERALL IMPROVEMENT FORMULA AND CALCULATION

$$\left(\frac{\text{Post-Assessment Total} - \text{Pre-Assessment Total}}{\text{Pre-Assessment Total}}\right) \times 100$$

$$\left(\frac{31-19}{19}\right) \times 100 \qquad (.6315) \times 100 = 63.15\%$$

30-MINUTE GROUPS: RELATIONSHIPS AND BELONGING

30-MINUTE GROUPS

CERTIFICATE
OF COMPLETION

This Certificate is Presented to:

For Participating in the **Realtionships and Belonging Group!**

Facilitator:

YOU ROCK!

RELATIONSHIPS AND BELONGING GROUP COMPLETION LETTER

Date:_____

Hello!

This week was the final session in our **Relationships and Belonging Group**! I am proud to say that your student has participated fully and has been presented with a Certificate of Completion.

Over the past ten sessions, we have reviewed the following topics:

- Understanding Your Strengths
- Appreciating the Value in Others
- Finding Where You Belong
- Achieving Wellness and Balance
- Defining Healthy Relationships
- Recognizing Unhealthy Relationships
- Protecting Your Worth
- Developing Consideration for Others
- Knowing Your Limits
- Respecting Others' Boundaries

If you have questions about the content of any of these topics, please ask your student to share with you what they have learned, or reach out to me at the school by email at any time during the school year.

Even though our group has ended, I am still available to them as needed. However, since we will no longer be meeting regularly, please don't hesitate to contact me with any questions or concerns that may come up.

I am incredibly proud of the students in this group and look forward to watching them learn and grow. Thank you so much for allowing them to participate in our **Relationships and Belonging Group**!

Warm regards,

_____
Facilitator's Name and Title

_____
Facilitator's Contact Information

REFERENCES

Bandura, A. (n.d.). *Social learning theory*. Simply Psychology. https://www.simplypsychology.org/bandura.html

Cherry, K. (2023). *Social learning theory: How people learn through observation*. Verywell Mind. https://www.verywellmind.com/social-learning-theory-2795074?print

Cacioppo, J. T., & Hawkley, L. C. (2009). Perceived social isolation and cognition. *Trends in Cognitive Sciences, 13*(10), 447–454. https://doi.org/10.1016/j.tics.2009.06.005

Domènech-Abella, J., Mundo, J., Haro, J. M., & Rubio-Valera, M. (2020). The role of perceived social support and cognitive function in the association between perceived social isolation and depression: A mediation analysis. *Social Psychiatry and Psychiatric Epidemiology, 55*(9), 1121–1129. https://doi.org/10.1007/s12160-010-9210-8

Santini, Z. I., Jose, P. E., Cornwell, E. Y., Koyanagi, A., Nielsen, L., Hinrichsen, C., Meilstrup, C., Madsen, K. R., & Koushede, V. (2020). Social disconnectedness, perceived isolation, and symptoms of depression and anxiety among older Americans (NSHAP): A longitudinal mediation analysis. *The Lancet Public Health, 5*(1), e62–e70. https://doi.org/10.1016/S2468-2667(19)30230-0

Silva, A. G. S., Silva, L. L. A., & de Andrade, C. P. (2022). Social isolation and its impact on adolescent mental health: A cross-sectional study. *Revista Paulista de Pediatria, 40*, e2020385. https://doi.org/10.1590/1984-0462/2022/40/2020385

Spreng, R. N., Dimas, E., Mwilambwe-Tshilobo, L., Dagher, A., Koellinger, P., Nave, G., Ong, A., Kernbach, J. M., Wiecki, T. V., Ge, T., Li, J., & Bzdok, D. (2020). The default network of the human brain is associated with perceived social isolation (Nature *Communications, 11*, Article 6393). https://doi.org/10.1038/s41467-020-20039-w

Wang, Y., Xu, D., Yan, S., & Tang, L. (2022). Early cognitive impairment and COVID-19 infection: A cohort study. *Journal of Cachexia, Sarcopenia and Muscle, 13*(1), 174–182. https://doi.org/10.1002/jcv2.12073

Young, L. J. (2011). Oxytocin, social cognition, and psychiatry. *Annals of the New York Academy of Sciences, 1224*(1), 162–173. https://doi.org/10.1111/j.1749-6632.2011.06028.x

---

THE RESOURCES IN THIS BOOK ARE AVAILABLE FOR YOU AS A DIGITAL DOWNLOAD!

Please visit **ncyi.org/downloadable-resources** to access the downloadable resources.

Enter the code below to unlock the resources:

RELATIONSHIPS593

ABOUT THE AUTHOR

Dr. Amy E. Baltimore, MEd, EdS, LPSC, NCC is a former missionary kid who grew up experiencing first hand what it is like to serve the needs of children with deep developmental trauma. With an undergraduate degree in musical theater and a masters degree in school counseling, she began her career by leaning into her passion for supporting the positive growth and development of students primarily in grades K-8 through musical theater programming and school counseling.

After 12 years of serving in schools as a school counselor, she realized the adults need just as much support as the students. So, after obtaining a specialist degree in Education Leadership, she stepped into the role of serving as a school counseling district leader and completed her personal educational journey by completing doctoral programming at Lipscomb University focused on the development of learning organizations, and strategic change.

Her professional experiences also include serving as Chair of the Board of Directors and legislative liaison for the Tennessee School Counselor Association, adjunct professor and frequent speaker at various higher ed events and state conferences, and advisory council for the Tennessee Department of Education school counseling department. Amy Baltimore is a Nationally Board Certified Counselor and a certified trainer for Restorative Practices, Building Strong Brains (ACEs/PCEs), The 6 Pillars of Trauma-Informed Schools, and Youth Mental Health First Aid.

Amy has been happily married for 26 years and has two amazing children who have grown and flown. She loves any activity involving sunshine and warm weather. On any given sunny day you can find her at the lake on her paddleboard, or on a bicycle riding the greenway, or hiking with her husband toward one of the many waterfalls found in middle Tennessee.

AMY'S SESSIONS

We're Not All Friends, and That's OK

Creating meaningful connections by understanding how our similarities and differences empower us, and realizing that setting healthy boundaries in relationships promotes mutual respect and understanding, reduces pressure and stress, and increases our confidence and ability to access personal growth.

Belonging: Valuing Self and Others

The cure for isolation and loneliness is learning to value yourself and people around you. Once you know your worth you can assign worth to others which leads to developing the ability to form relationships that heal.

Demystifying Advocacy for School Counselors

Your voice matters! As a school counselor you can lean into the ASCA National Model and additional resources to become a strong advocate for each and every student at your local school level, the district level, and even the state level.

Empowering the School Counselor and Administrator Relationship

What do school counselors need to get their programs off the ground – administrators! What do administrators need to fill the gaps for student support – school counselors! The two go hand in hand. Through the strategic use of data to close gaps in student outcomes, collaboration between the school counselor and school administrator yields improved results for student academic achievement, attendance, and social behavior.

The Crisis of Change: From Surviving to Thriving

If there is one constant in education today, it is "change." Change is inevitable and we can't seem to escape it; so how do we lean into it and do more than just survive the onslaught? Here we will lay it all out on the table and openly discuss the crises and conflicts we encounter when change occurs, then we will grapple with some ways to engage with the change and come out the other side thriving in our work as educators.

30-MINUTE GROUPS

30MinuteGroups.com

BONUS! Includes Downloadable Resources and Templates!

Scan here for more 30-MINUTE GROUPS RESOURCES

30-Minute Groups is a new curriculum series that aims to help school counselors and educators navigate three main challenges they encounter when attempting to start a small group:

- Workload Demands to manage the number of students for whom they are responsible
- No Prep Time to create lessons and activities for small group sessions
- Budget Constraints for ongoing training

The strategic design allows students to empathize, connect with others, and translate their new knowledge into practice. The American School Counselor Association (ASCA®)-aligned curriculum contains an introductory lesson, ten core topical lessons, and a completion session. Practical and applicable, the activities provided are suitable for small and large group instruction and require no additional materials!

Visit 30MinuteGroups.com for our latest additions to the series!

About NCYI

National Center for Youth Issues provides educational resources, training, and support programs to foster the healthy social, emotional, and physical development of children and youth. Since our founding in 1981, NCYI has established a reputation as one of the country's leading providers of teaching materials and training for counseling and student-support professionals. NCYI helps meet the immediate needs of students throughout the nation by ensuring those who mentor them are well prepared to respond across the developmental spectrum.

Connect With Us Online!

@nationalcenterforyouthissues

@ncyi

@nationalcenterforyouthissues